Paranormal
SURREY

Paranormal SURREY

RUPERT MATTHEWS

The
History
Press

First published 2010

The History Press
The Mill, Brimscombe Port
Stroud, Gloucestershire, GL5 2QG
www.thehistorypress.co.uk

British Library Cataloguing in Publication Data.
A catalogue record for this book is available from the British Library.

ISBN 978 0 7524 5422 1

Typesetting and origination by The History Press
Printed in Great Britain

CONTENTS

INTRODUCTION

Surrey is one of the most charming of English counties, with a surprisingly wide variety of landscapes, towns and villages to attract both residents and outsiders.

There are the high downs stretching across the county from east to west. The bare chalk grasslands that crown these hills have offered grazing to sheep for centuries, and more recently have attracted the owners of racehorses. The races held on the downs at Epsom are among the most popular in the world – especially the Derby held every June. North of the downs are extensive sandy heaths interspersed with shallow river valleys that run down to the Thames to form the county's northern border. South of the downs are the wide, low-lying forests of the Weald.

Of course, much of this natural landscape has been built over in the past century or so. Some already established towns such as Dorking, Reigate or Guildford have expanded across neighbouring open country. Other towns are entirely modern – there was very little at either Redhill or Woking until a railway was built linking them to London in the Victorian period.

But no amount of building or modernisation can hide the paranormal face of this county. There are ghosts, monsters and poltergeists to be found here, perhaps rather more than in most counties. If the hairy monster of Reigate's Shag Brook has not been seen for a good few years, the Surrey Puma continues to be seen with regularity. The ghosts of Surrey are an active lot; they crop up along roadsides, in pubs, around churches and in houses. Generally they seem content to potter about their business without taking too much notice of the humans that share their county. And Surrey also plays host to UFOs, poltergeists, apparitions and the little people.

Surrey may wear a face of suburban and rural normality, but lurking not far below the surface is a paranormal county of unequalled strangeness and activity.

ONE

ANCIENT MONSTERS

Surrey is a famously suburban county. It lies just on the south-western edge of London, and over the years much of what was once Surrey countryside has been swallowed up by the sprawling housing and factories of the capital and now lies under the jurisdiction of the London authorities. Beyond the reach of London itself, much of the county is covered by housing estates, towns and villages.

But it was not always this way. Only a couple of centuries ago, Surrey was a rural place with extensive tracts of woodland where few humans ventured other than foresters and charcoal burners. It was in these forests that there were said to be unusual beasts and terrifying monsters of various kinds.

It doesn't look much today, but the small stream west of Reigate known as Shag Brook was once the haunt of a ferocious water monster that gobbled up unwary travellers and terrified the locals beyond reason.

Stories about the monster are common in old books about Surrey. One tells of a Reigate lad who joined a cavalry regiment to fight Napoleon's French armies in the early nineteenth century. Returning home on leave, the lad had grown into a strapping trooper with a wealth of tales about his courage. Late one evening, after a particularly boastful tale over a mug of ale, the soldier's more timid friends who had stayed at home to farm laid a hefty wager that he would not ride to Buckland and back, crossing the fateful stream. The soldier trotted out bravely enough, but came back at the gallop with a white face and trembling hands. He collected his wager, but never again dared to cross the Shag Brook after dark.

He reported that the journey had begun well. He had rode out of Reigate heading west, along what is now the A25, seeing his way by starlight. As he approached the stream, however, the horse had shied. Peering ahead in the darkness, the man could see nothing. He therefore urged the horse on and after something of a struggle, he got it to splash through the shallow ford and out the other side. A strange silence then fell, as if the forest was holding its breath.

Nervous now, the bold soldier turned his horse's head back toward Reigate and urged it forward. This time the horse walked forward calmly enough until it was in the stream. Then something caught the soldier's eye. He turned to stare at the movement and saw perched on a rock by the stream a terrifying sight. Squatting on its haunches and glaring at him malevolently was what looked like a naked man covered in dense hair or fur. The shoulders and arms of the strange creature bulged with muscles that appeared to be enormously strong. The apparition was topped off by an ape-like head. The brows were low and heavy, the mouth pushed forward in an animal snout and the eyes were deep set and small. The beast opened its mouth to reveal powerful teeth that protruded forward like great tusks.

At that moment, the beast sprang forwards toward the terrified soldier. The man slammed his spurs into his horse, which leapt forward with a start. The soldier felt a heavy weight land on the horse behind him and a pair of powerful arms seized him from behind. He swore that he could feel the hot breath of the monster on his neck and certainly caught the fetid stench of a carnivore in his nostrils. Fearing at any moment to feel the razor sharp teeth plunge into his flesh, the soldier spurred forwards. Then the beast was gone, presumably having leapt off to return to its watery home. The soldier did not draw rein until he got back to the pub. No wonder he would never return to the Shag Brook.

A few years later, a farmer was returning to Reigate after delivering a load of corn to Dorking. It was evening, but not yet dark, when he approached the stream, so he was not worried. On reaching the brook his horses halted and no amount of whipping or leading could persuade them to move forward. The horses were shaking with fear and finally backed off and stared with terrified eyes at the steam, seeing something the farmer could not.

An answer to the nature of this monstrous beast may be found in the name of the stream: the Shag Brook. The word Shag is closely related to Shuck and Strike, both names given to mysterious monsters elsewhere in England. The words seem to be derived from the Anglo-Saxon for a demon or evil spirit. Furthermore, the description of the monster closely matches that of Grendel, the half-man half-monster who also lived in water. Grendel was fought by the legendary Anglo-Saxon hero Beowulf in an eighth-century epic poem.

So was there a dreadful water monster lurking west of Reigate, or were the stories just the dimly-remembered echoes of a pre-Christian, Anglo-Saxon demon story? Sadly we shall probably never know. The Shag was said to lurk beside a large upright stone which stood on the banks of the brook. This stone had a red mark down the side of it that could not be removed by any amount of scrubbing or pounding. It was consequently known as the Bleeding Stone.

In the mid-nineteenth century, the local landowner had the stone removed to quell the superstitious tales about the monster. For a time, the Bleeding Stone was a feature of the gardens of Buckland Court, but it does not seem to be there any longer. The beast has not been seen since the stone was moved. Yet.

Another monster that may have been a mythical beast, or just possibly a real living animal, was the creature that once frequented the area around West Clandon. Descriptions of this monster are, if anything, even vaguer than those of the Farnham Cat that we will meet shortly. It favoured the damp meadows north of the village, alongside the stream that flows north to enter the Wey near Newark. It drank from a spring in the woodland known today as Frythys Wood. It is variously described as being a 'serpent', a 'worm' or a 'scaled beast'.

Those who favour a rational explanation for this beast portray it as being a large snake. The idea put forward is that it was a type of python brought back from India by some returning merchant or soldier that had escaped into the wild and taken up residence at West Clandon. The Indian python can grow to be over 20ft long and would certainly have been a fearsome sight to Surrey folk accustomed only to seeing the odd adder or grass snake. On the other hand, the python is adapted to the hot climate of India, and would have been hard pushed to survive a chilly Surrey winter.

The narrow Shag Brook flows through woodland south of the modern main road at Buckland. In years gone by, a horrific monster awaited travellers at the ford through the stream.

The village sign at West Clandon commemorates the legendary encounter between a dog and a fearsome dragon that took place here some centuries ago.

Others have suggested that the West Clandon beast was a dragon or similar legendary monster. Whether such creatures ever actually existed or not is open to question, but they certainly feature in numerous local legends across England. Some people believe that the many tales of dragons were inspired by distorted memories of some real, large animal that was encountered by the ancestors of those who told the tales: the woolly mammoth, cave lion or giant bear which lived in Britain until around 14,000 years ago, perhaps. Others think that the idea of a dragon was inspired by dinosaur bones discovered by chance.

Whatever the truth, the story as told in West Clandon is that the fearsome serpent killed and ate anything that came its way. Given that its lair lay not far from the main road, now the A247, this was something of a problem for the local folk. The beast terrorised the district for many years, consuming livestock and the occasional human to keep itself going.

Then one day a mournful procession came to the village. It consisted of a small detachment of Redcoat soldiers, led by a captain and a dejected private whose hands were bound and who was firmly tied to the officer's horse. At the heels of the captive trotted a small dog, a terrier. The small group arrived in the evening and set up camp just outside the Onslow Arms inn. It soon transpired that the captive soldier was a man who had deserted his regiment on active service abroad and who was being taken back to the regiment's home base for trial and – it was widely expected by the other soldiers – execution.

When the villagers told the soldiers of their local dragon, the captain was inclined not to believe them. The captive, however, perked up. He announced that he had fought just such a dragon before and knew how to defeat it. He offered to rid the village of its monster, but only on condition that the captain promised that he would be released and absolved of his crime should he be successful. The captain was reluctant, trusting in neither the story of a dragon nor the trustworthiness of the culprit once he was untied. Eventually, however, he was persuaded.

Next morning the released soldier set off north from the village to the lair of the dragon. He took with him his dog, a musket and bayonet and a single shot. It was, he said, all that he would need. The other soldiers and some of the hardier villagers followed at a safe distance.

The dragon was found to be resting beside the spring where it liked to drink. The soldier approached carefully to within a few feet of the slumbering giant. He then fired his musket into the air, waking the serpent and causing it to rush toward him. The dog promptly sprang forward to seize the monster by the tail. This sudden pain caused the beast to rear up, exposing its vulnerable belly, into which the solder thrust the bayonet to inflict a single, fatal wound. The monster fell dead.

The captain was true to his word and released the soldier, who chose to settle down among the grateful villagers of West Clandon and take up his old occupation as a farmer. The spring where the monster was killed was renamed Dead Well – it is still there – and peace returned to the area.

Rather more realistic was the beast that was seen roaming the woods and fields around Farnham in the 1770s. The creature preferred the more wooded areas, and was usually seen as it climbed a tree or scampered into dense cover to escape the human intruder that disturbed it. The most typical description given of this animal is that it was a very large, cat-like creature. Some said that it was as big as a hound, others estimated it was larger still. Everyone agreed that it had a grey or silver coat with mottled markings.

One man who saw the mysterious creature at fairly close quarters later joined the Army and saw service in Canada. While in New Brunswick, he came across a creature that he thought looked very like the strange cat at Farnham. The only difference that he could see was that the Canadian cat had a shorter tail. The animal in question was the North American lynx, which grows to be about 4ft 6in long.

If the Farnham Cat was a real creature, what exactly was it? Given the eyewitness testimony that it greatly resembled a North American lynx, the most obvious answer is that it was a European lynx. However, that species is not native to Britain and even in those areas of Europe where it does live, it does not favour woodland near towns and villages but prefers remote upland areas.

It has been suggested that the Farnham Cat was instead a European wildcat. This creature does live in Britain, though not in Surrey, and so one might just conceivably have wandered far from its native home to seek prey in the Surrey woods. The wildcat is, however, less than half the size of a lynx and so would have been too small to be the mystery animal. Moreover, it has striped tabby markings, not splotches of colour.

A very different sort of monster once lurked on the hills just east of Churt. These hills are highly distinctive, being a line of three sharp, steep hills that rise out of the otherwise fairly level common land to a height of 375ft. It was none other than the Devil himself who frequented these hills. For reasons best known to himself, the Evil One enjoyed jumping from one hilltop to the next and back again. Whenever he came to Surrey, the Devil would leap about on the hills, thus giving them their name of the Devil's Jumps.

The ancient pagan god Thor features in the stories about the Devil's Jumps and the blacksmith of Thursley. He is also shown on the village sign.

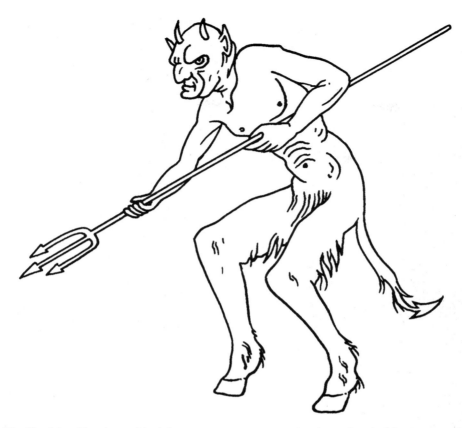

The Devil is said to have visited Surrey many years ago, and to have played a bizarre game that had unforeseen consequences on the hills near Churt.

Just two miles to the east, in Thursley, lived a blacksmith named Thunor. This Thunor was prodigiously strong, but he did like his sleep. And when the Devil came at night, the sounds of the jumping kept the blacksmith awake. One night it all got too much for him. Thunor came tearing out of his house in a terrible rage. Seeing a huge boulder by the roadside, he lifted it up and hurled it at the Devil. The rock struck the Devil in the chest and sent him sprawling in ungainly fashion. So surprised was the Devil by this blow that he raced off back to Hell and never again came to the hills between Churt and Thursley.

It is an interesting tale, made more fascinating by the fact that the village of Thursley derives its name from the Old English 'Thunor's Leagh'. A leagh was a grove of trees. However, Thunor was no blacksmith, but instead the pagan god Thunor – the English equivalent of the Viking Thor. The pagan English liked to worship their gods in sacred clearings or groves, and there can be no doubt that Thursley was one such pagan holy place. Quite how the pagan warrior god Thunor got into conflict with the arch demon of the Christian religion we can only guess at.

All these monsters and demons, whether real or imagined, have long since passed away from Surrey. But that is not to say that mysterious creatures are no longer roaming the countryside. If the stories are to be believed, they are here still.

TWO

MODERN MONSTERS

With its mass of gardens filled with fruit trees, berry shrubs and other tasty treats for birds and small mammals, Surrey is richer in wildlife than many other English counties. That wildlife is, of course, fairly small and entirely harmless to man. Magpies, squirrels, blue tits, hedgehogs and a variety of finches are familiar visitors to most gardens. Foxes have been famously moving into suburban areas to scavenge from bins, feast on takeaway food scraps and hunt down mice or birds. In more rural areas, Surrey gardens play host to badgers, which at 3ft long are the largest wild animals native to Surrey.

Of course, there was a time when rather more formidable animals roamed the Surrey countryside. Wolves were common in medieval times and bears roamed the forests a few centuries earlier. However, the idea that dangerous animals such as these might still be roaming the county would strike most residents as not only somewhat disturbing, but also ridiculous. Yet there are persistent reports that a species of animal that is famously unpredictable and violent is indeed making its home in the county: the Surrey Puma.

Interestingly, the very earliest reports of a large cat-like creature at large in Surrey came from Farnham. This was close to where the mysterious Farnham Cat was seen in the later eighteenth century. This latter's arrival was, however, rather larger and potentially more dangerous than the earlier lynx-like animal. At the time, the early reports were not much publicised and quickly forgotten.

The reports were made by local residents, who said that they had encountered a large cat-like beast in the fields south and east of the town. The most detailed came from a man driving along a lane at dusk when an animal sprang down from a bank into the road about 50yds ahead of him. The man slammed on his brakes to watch the creature cross the road. The animal seemed to be about the size of a Labrador dog, but moved in a distinctly cat-like way. The car came to a halt as the creature bounded off the road into the shade of a tree. The driver wound down his window to inspect the animal as it stood still, apparently watching some sheep in an adjacent field. He noted a thick tail that curled up toward the end, pointed ears and a clearly cat-like head. After a while, the animal trotted off into woodland and was lost to view.

The police carried out a cursory search of the area, but found nothing to indicate that a big cat was on the loose. The reports were logged, but no further action was taken. It was only later that anyone took any notice of these incidents and wondered if they were the first appearance of the Surrey Puma.

On 16 July 1962 the big cat was reported again. The witness this time was Ernest Jellett, a worker employed by the Mid–Wessex Water Board to look after the various lands that it owned around reservoirs, treatment works and the like. It was fairly early in the morning as Jellett got out of his van to walk up a track through woodland that surrounded the Heathy Park Reservoir near Farnham.

Jellett had not gone far when he saw a rabbit nibbling the grass beside the track some yards ahead of him. He stopped to watch, and then spotted a much larger creature in the undergrowth beyond the rabbit. The vegetation obscured the animal, but it was obviously much larger than a fox and was clearly stalking the rabbit. At this point, the rabbit spotted Jellett and turned back toward the undergrowth, obviously unaware that a greater danger lay in that direction.

That was when the large animal leapt out to attack. It missed the rabbit, which bolted down the track toward Jellett. The larger creature gave chase after the rabbit. When the rabbit jinked to one side off the track into long grass, the hunter continued straight on toward Jellett. From being merely curious, Jellett now became suddenly alarmed. The animal racing toward him was a substantial beast that looked like nothing so much as a small lion. It had a tawny or sandy coat of short fur and a long tail that was thin along its entire length, not bushy like that of a fox. The head was round and the face fairly flat, like that of a cat. And the teeth were clearly those of a hunter.

Jellett had no weapon on him, not so much as a stick or wrench. He shouted loudly, waving his arms about in an attempt to frighten off the unknown animal that was running at him. The creature responded by turning aside and bounding off into the undergrowth. After a few seconds of rustling vegetation, silence returned and Jellett was left alone.

Shaken by his experience, Jellett walked back to his van, keeping a careful watch on the surroundings. He drove quickly to a phone box and called the police to report a dangerous animal on the loose. The police responded with speed and were soon searching the woodland around Heathy Park Reservoir. They did not find the mystery animal, but they did discover signs that it had not been a figment of Jellett's imagination. There was a patch of bracken where some large animal had lain down to rest.

Worried that something was on the loose in western Surrey, the police asked locals to keep an eye open for signs of anything unusual. Less than a week later a farmer called to say that his cattle had been behaving oddly. For over an hour the previous evening, they had been milling around and lowing loudly as if frightened by something. He had thought a stray dog was worrying them and gone out in search of it, but had seen nothing. The cattle continued to be uneasy for some time before settling down again.

A couple of days later a woman phoned in to say that she had encountered a strange creature near Crondall, just over the county border in Hampshire. She had been out walking her dog when she spotted the creature. The woman had been able to watch it for some time before it sensed her presence and ran off. She had hurried home and consulted a book on wild animals. Knowing that what she had seen was not native to Britain, the woman had flicked through the entire book. The picture that she thought was closest to the thing she had seen was of a South American cat called the jaguarundi. This cat has a smooth coat of uniform colour, ranging from almost black through tawny to russet. It is about 3ft long and features a distinctively cat-like head and face.

Once again the reports tailed off. After making a few enquiries, the police gave up the hunt for the mysterious big cat, filed the reports and got back to their primary business of catching criminals.

However, the big cat had not gone away. This time it remained the subject of talk and gossip in the pubs and shops of western Surrey and north-eastern Hampshire. One man in particular kept up an interest. Edward Blanks of Bushylease Farm, near Crondall, had himself seen the big cat – though only fleetingly – and he had found pugmarks left in soft mud by the creature as it prowled around. It seemed to be in the area only during the later spring and summer, presumably moving off to other feeding grounds at other times of year. On occasion, Blanks and his adult son detected a fetid stench that they put down to the mysterious intruder.

In August 1964, Blanks was alarmed to find that his herd of pedigree Frisian cattle had stampeded, broken their way out of their field and were scattered through adjacent woodland and fields for some considerable distance. Obviously something had frightened them very badly, but the most immediate problem was to get the animals rounded up and safely back where they should be. It was while gathering the cattle that Blanks' son found one cow that was bleeding from some severe and very odd injuries.

A vet was summoned, who stitched up the wounds. He was puzzled. The wounds had clearly not been made by a dog – the usual culprit in such circumstances – and were severe enough to indicate that whatever had attacked the cow could easily despatch a calf or sheep. The vet was of the opinion that no animal native to Britain, nor any breed of dog, could have inflicted the injuries.

The wounded cow was photographed for the local newspaper, which sold the story on to the national media. Suddenly the tale of a big cat on the loose in the Home Counties was national news. The beast was dubbed with various titles: the Crondall Cougar or the Phantom Cat, but it was the name Surrey Puma which stuck.

Among those who read the press reports was Billy Davidson, a Canadian ranger who happened to be on holiday in England at the time. He had neither his hunting rifle, nor a British permit to use anything similar, but he still phoned Blanks to offer his help. Blanks accepted and Davidson came down to Crondall to scout out the territory around Bushylease Farm. After a couple of days probing the countryside, Davidson announced that he was convinced that a puma was in the neighbourhood. He said that he had found unmistakable signs of the big cat, including a characteristic laying-up lair.

The puma, also known as the cougar or mountain lion, is a large cat native to the Americas, from southern Canada through the USA, Mexico and Central America to the Andes. There are several local varieties of the species, varying substantially in colour and size, but the overall appearance and habits of the cat are fairly uniform. An adult may be anything from 3ft to 6ft long, with a tail of up to 3ft in length adding to that. It usually lives alone, coming together only to mate or if a mother keeps young adults by her side.

The puma is usually active around dusk and dawn, preferring to lie up in dense cover during daylight hours. If hungry, however, it may come out to hunt at any time of the day or night. The prey it favours in its home ranges varies from rats and hares up to deer. It has been known to attack domestic cattle in the Americas, but this is rare and only calves are hunted with any real success. The thought that such a creature was on the loose in Surrey was extremely disturbing.

Where such a creature could have come from was a question on everyone's lips. A favoured early theory was that the cat had escaped from a circus or zoo. It was soon proved that no large cat had been lost from any such establishment. The next theory was that a private collector had lost a big cat. Owning a large, dangerous animal is now illegal without a licence, but in the

1960s this was not the case – though the number of people who did collect such animals was very small. All those known to trade or collect large animals were contacted, and none said that they had any big cat missing. Of course, they might have been covering up an escape in case they were found liable for any damage the animal caused.

In all there were twenty-three pumas known to be in Britain in 1964. Every single one of them was accounted for. It was possible that a puma could have been smuggled in illegally, but those who dealt in large cats maintained that this was unlikely. As the law then existed, there was no real financial incentive to smuggle a big cat into Britain when they could be imported legally with ease.

With no obvious source for a big cat on the loose, some began to question if the creature really existed. Perhaps it had been a big dog that attacked the cattle after all. But the sightings continued.

Several people in the Crondall-Farnham area reported seeing a big cat in late August. All these sightings were at a distance and could be dismissed by sceptics as misidentified dogs and domestic cats, although the witnesses themselves were adamant about what they had seen. Then in early September, George Wisdom was out picking blackberries on Munstead Heath, near Godalming. He was quietly picking berries from the exterior of a dense thicket when he was rooted to the spot by a terrifying snarl. Whatever had made the noise was very close and clearly very angry. Wisdom froze for a moment, staring around in fear to try to locate the source of the noise. He decided that it had come from inside the thicket and began to back away as quietly as he could. A second noise came that was decidedly less angry and convinced Wisdom that he was taking the correct action. He continued to back away, trying to judge when would be the best moment to turn and run. Suddenly a large creature sprang out of the thicket. Much to Wisdom's relief, it was heading away from him. The beast turned to look at him for an instant, then ran off.

The frightened berry picker hurried to report the encounter. He gave one of the most detailed descriptions of the Surrey Puma to emerge in 1964. He gave an almost textbook description of a puma, right down to the dark tip to the tail and vertical pale lines under the eyes. If Wisdom's account was to be trusted, there could now be no doubt at all about what was on the loose in Surrey: it was a puma.

A few days later, a racehorse trainer bringing his charges out to exercise in the early morning found a set of footprints on the raked sand track that he owned. The line of prints ran for almost half a mile and each mark was about 6in across. Plaster casts were taken of some of the clearer prints and sent to London Zoo for analysis. Again the identification was clear: puma. However, experts did warn against fraud. Wild animal tracks are not that difficult to imitate if a person has the right equipment and knows what they are doing.

In the early evening of 28 September 1964, a woman reported seeing a puma at Witley. Then, in the summer of 1965, a teenage boy was walking over fields near Kenley Airfield when he heard something large moving through the undergrowth of a nearby wood. The boy stopped as the noise grew closer. Then a large cat sprang out of the wood and came running toward him. He recalled later that the animal was about the size of an Alsatian dog, but was definitely cat-like in its movements and appearance. He was rooted to the spot in fear, but the creature loped on past him and vanished over a hedge. He thought that he saw the cat again, keeping pace with him by stalking through long grass. He took to his heels and fled.

In August 1966, a puma was sighted in a garden at Cutt Mill and again at Wormley a few days later in another garden.

The police were by this point convinced that they were dealing with a real flesh and blood puma or similar big cat. A large metal cage was installed at Godalming Police Station and an RSPCA inspector brought in to give policemen advice on how best to tackle a puma should they come across one. A formal log book was opened in which all sightings of a big cat, records of pugmarks or details of attacks on livestock were recorded. Many of the entries were inconclusive or lacking in detail, and a few were subsequently proved to have been of a dog, but others were clear and precise.

However, no puma or cougar was caught. As the months slipped by, public interest outside of Surrey and Hampshire began to wane. There were plenty of sightings and prints, but this was just more of the same and the media began to tire of the story. Locally, it was a different story. Living in close proximity to a cougar is an experience that not many people wanted. People began to want the mystery cleared up.

In 1966, a group of naturalists organised a Surrey safari in an effort to track the beast down. They failed to find the Surrey Puma. That same summer an experienced big game hunter attempted to locate it, but with a similarly negative result. Even a Boy Scout troop tried its luck. By 1967, the efforts had a less serious atmosphere. A pub began selling fake 'Big Game Permits' to would-be hunters, with proceeds going to a local charity.

Those who were sceptical that a big cat could be on the loose and surviving in Surrey began to point out that there was a lack of hard physical evidence. Apart from sightings – which could always be cases of mistaken identity or simply invented – there were only a few footprints, and they too could be faked fairly easily. The injuries suffered by livestock might have provided some evidence. Undoubtedly the majority of killings and injuries reported to police were inflicted by dogs. It is amazing how the owners of domestic dogs simply refuse to believe that their beloved pet might attack an animal similar to the dog's natural prey. Much suffering by farm animals is caused by thoughtless dog owners who let their dogs off the leash on farmland.

There were some injuries that were different from the usual run of dog attacks. There were a few that were so abnormal that they were subjected to inspection by a Ministry of Agriculture expert. That expert pronounced that the injuries were 'outside the previous experience' of the ministry. The report stopped short of identifying the wounds as being made by a puma for the simple reason that none of the experts had ever seen a puma attack victim and so had nothing to compare the injuries to.

In August 1966, a photo was taken near Worplesdon that was claimed to be of the Surrey Puma. Although it undoubtedly shows a puma-like figure, the photo has nothing in it to provide scale. The figure might be 6ft long or 1ft long – it is impossible to tell. The photographer said it was very big, but that has no more validity than an eyewitness report. The newspapers sent the picture to specialists at Chessington Zoo, London Zoo and the Natural History Museum. The London Zoo said there was not enough detail to identify the creature, but both Chessington Zoo and the Natural History Museum replied that they thought the photo showed a puma.

In 1968 a rumour raced around Surrey that a farmer had shot the elusive puma with a shotgun and killed it. No body was ever produced to support the rumour, but it was a convenient time for the police to close down the formal investigation. Reports of a puma continued to be made to the Surrey police, and they were still logged, but so far as the police were concerned it was none of their business.

At the height of the hunt for the Surrey Puma, a large steel cage was installed at Godalming Police Station, ready to hold the savage cat just as soon as somebody might be able to capture it.

A puma, photographed in North America by Steve Jurvetson. The descriptions given by those who claim to have seen a big cat in Surrey usually conform to this species.

The open links of Bramley Golf Club were the venue for a classic sighting of the Surrey Puma.

Despite this official dismissal, the Surrey Puma stubbornly refused to vanish. In the summer of 1969, a line of tracks was found in the sand of a bunker at the Bramley Golf Club. A plaster cast was taken and the prints were identified as those of a big cat. In December 1970, a line of big cat tracks were found in snow at Farnborough.

The reports of a large cat-like creature continued to be made over the years. In 1995 Steve Ashcroft, a policeman from Bookham, was travelling to work when he saw what he was convinced was a puma chasing a roe deer on Bookham Common.

On 6 January 1998, Jill Mussett of Cranleigh sighted what she thought was a puma in the field behind her house. She grabbed a pair of binoculars and focussed on the animal. She reported that it had 'lovely, sleek chocolate brown fur, gorgeous green eyes and pointed ears, with a long, sleek tail turned up at the end. It was about the size of a Labrador but much sleeker. Its movements were certainly cat-like.'

In 2003, two Kingston police officers reported seeing a large black beast which ran across the road in front of them. In 2004, Bruce Burgess of Leatherhead was out surveying sites for a pond at Brook Willow Farm when he saw a very large brown or tawny cat trotting across a field. He had a camera and managed to snap off a few photos of the mysterious animal. Unfortunately, the creature was so far away that the pictures came out slightly out of focus and too indistinct to be considered as evidence.

On 16 April 2005, a woman and a friend spotted a huge black cat at the bottom of her garden in Ewell. They later likened it to a black leopard. On 26 August 2008, Howard Jackson woke up early at a camp site in East Horsley. He decided to go for an early morning stroll down to the adjacent lake and spotted a very large, sandy-coloured cat walking silently and smoothly along the water's edge. He estimated that the creature was about as big as a Labrador dog, but that it had a cat-shaped head and moved with the slinky walk of a feline. When the animal spotted Jackson it slipped off into undergrowth. A few weeks later, on 1 October, Peter Broadbent was in Browns Lane, Effingham, talking to a friend when he saw 'a large, light coloured, cat-type creature about the size of a Labrador' moving across the adjacent sports field.

All the early investigators of the Surrey Puma were convinced that they were dealing with a single live puma. As time passed, however, opinions began to differ. Some investigators came to the conclusion that there was no puma at all. They thought that eyewitnesses were either mistaken in what they had seen or had made the whole thing up. Given the weight of evidence, this seems unlikely.

Others began to think that there was not one puma, but several. A single puma could not survive from 1962 to 2008, so it was suggested that there was a breeding pair with cubs growing to adulthood. However, if it was stretching credulity that one puma could live for years in a county as densely inhabited as Surrey without leaving behind firm evidence, the idea that half a dozen could do so seems ridiculous.

A few researchers began to wonder if the creature being seen was actually a flesh and blood puma at all. The antics of the Surrey Puma were seen to resemble certain paranormal apparitions, such as ghosts, Black Shuck, owl men and such like from around the world. Some suggested that whatever enigmatic force was behind these apparitions had also produced the Surrey Puma. The fact that many sightings took place on or close to ley lines was put forward to support a paranormal origin for the cat. Other researchers postulated – though admittedly without much evidence – that UFOs were behind it all.

In the final analysis, nobody really knows what the Surrey Puma was, or is. All we do know is that something odd is being seen slinking around the county. Something has been attacking livestock. And whatever that something is, it is still there.

THREE

HIGHWAY GHOSTS

Ghosts, phantoms, spooks, spectres – call them what you will, but these apparitions crop up all over the place. They are found in churches, homes, factories, shops and roaming the countryside. Some of them have long and complex stories attached to them; others are anonymous phantoms that have no known background. And for some peculiar reason, in Surrey these spirits are encountered on roads and byways rather more often than anywhere else in the kingdom.

The phantom which haunts Cobham Bridge over the River Mole is something of a mystery. Nobody knows who it is, when the hauntings began or what the phantom tries to achieve. But on one thing all witnesses agree with absolute certainty; the ghost is of an incredibly ugly man.

One man who saw the ghost a few years ago reported:

I was driving into Cobham from Guildford with my girlfriend late on Saturday afternoon. As we approached the bridge we saw a tall man standing beside the road. I noticed him because he had a dark coat on, which I thought odd as it was a hot day. Then he began running towards us. I thought perhaps he wanted us to stop, so I began to slow down. I could see him very clearly. He had longish dark hair and a great big hooked nose. He really was an ugly bloke. When we got about 40yds from him, he just vanished. One second he was there, the next he was gone. Weird.

It seems the unfortunate phantom of Cobham Bridge is doomed to remain in anonymity. Nobody knows his name and those who see him often don't realise he is a ghost. And the one thing he is known for he could probably do without. Because he really is terribly ugly.

The other roadside ghost at Cobham is quite different. She is the phantom of a rather pretty young lady of about twenty years of age. Even so, most people would rather not encounter her. She stands beside the Portsmouth Road as it starts to dip down into the village from the north-east coming from Esher. The phantom is usually seen in late evening when the weather is unkind; rain seems to be her favourite. She appears to be flagging down passing cars as if wanting a lift. Those that do stop to offer her a lift are usually bemused to find that she has vanished. Why would a girl be waving cars to a stop, only to run off? Because she is a phantom of course.

The story most often attached to this spectre is that she is the ghost of an unfortunate Cobham woman who at some date in the 1950s went to the pub then known as the Tartar, later the Saracen's Head and which is now no longer in existence. She left the pub fairly late to find that it was raining and so she flagged down a passing motorist to hitch a lift home. She got home safely enough to her house near the church, but was then killed in a raging fire that broke out in the small hours of the morning. Presumably her ghost is recreating her last few hours on earth, though why it should focus on getting a lift is unclear.

At least one motorist has claimed that he actually gave the ghost a lift. He says that she sat pale and trembling in his car all the way from the Portsmouth Road through to Church Street, where she got out without a word of thanks and walked off into the night. He says that throughout this experience he had thought that there was something a bit odd about the girl, but that he had taken her for a real human. It was not until he was discussing the event later and was told of the ghost that he realised the truth of his encounter.

Quite different again is the jovial ghost which totters along the towpath north of Kingston town centre. He grins happily at everyone he meets. But how then did he become a ghost?

One witness who met this phantom on the towpath in 1989 said:

At first I thought he was someone in fancy dress and a bit the worse for wear, but when he got closer I realised there was something odd about him. He wasn't making any sound! He was obviously having a great time, laughing and singing as he staggered along. But he was totally silent. He was a big chap, taller than me (which would have put him around 6ft tall) and broad. He was dressed like a Cavalier from the Civil War days.

The bridge over the River Mole at Cobham is the home of a phantom that deeply disturbs those who see him, but not for reasons that might be expected.

Just who this jolly chap might be is not clear. He is, however, usually associated with Ham House, as his route from Kingston is clearly heading for that mansion. Originally a quiet country retreat, Ham House was massively enlarged and embellished in the 1670s by the Duke of Lauderdale – and the character of this nobleman gives a clue to the origins of our ghost.

Lauderdale was a staunch Royalist who spent most of the years of Cromwell's rule in prison. He was given high office by King Charles II when he regained his throne, but was never popular. Lauderdale was a sternly religious man who preferred the business of government to the luxuries of Charles's Court. Lauderdale's wife, however, was a more fun-loving sort who gathered a lively set of friends around her. Elizabeth Vivasour had brought Ham House as part of her dowry and she loved the house.

It can be guessed that when the Duke came to Ham his wife's rowdy friends had to be on best behaviour. If they needed to find some fun it would have been only natural if they headed for the nearest town: Kingston. At the time, Kingston was a busy river port, market town and, perhaps most important, a brewing centre. The Rowles Brewery in Brook Street had been founded in 1600 and at one point was producing 1½ million gallons of beer a year. No doubt the more fun-loving souls from Ham House came here for nightly revelry.

The old Portsmouth Road as it enters Cobham near the old Tartar pub, now a housing development. The ghost of a pretty young woman has been seen here trying to hitch a lift, but motorists who stop for her are in for a shock.

The towpath alongside the River Thames north of Kingston town centre is haunted by a most jovial spirit.

So maybe the jolly towpath phantom was one of the Duchess Elizabeth's friends on his way back from a drunken spree in Kingston. Perhaps, as he staggered home along the poorly-lit towpath, he tripped and pitched into the dark waters of the Thames. If so, his ghost could be retracing his last earthly journey. Whoever he was and whatever he was doing, our ghost was clearly enjoying himself.

Much less is known about the ghostly lady of Seven Hills Road, a road that runs from Cobham to Weybridge. This phantom is usually said to be that of an old lady dressed in a grey cloak or coat. She waits beside the road near the junction with Chestnut Avenue. As a car or van approaches she suddenly steps out, causing the driver to slam on the brakes. There is never any collision and when the driver steps out to investigate, the woman has gone without a trace.

Equally enigmatic, but rather more sinister, is the old lady of West Street in Farnham. This old lady walks with a quick and determined step along West Street, heading away from the town centre toward Wrecclesham. Also seen in the same street, and also heading in the same direction, is a different spook: a large black dog. The folk of Farnham have no legends handed down about this dog, but from his appearance and habits he sounds very similar to the phantom known in other parts of England as Shuck, Skeff or Scarf. This great black hound is said to be remarkably strong and to have considerable magical powers. It is generally thought to be a creature of malevolence and that if it looks at you with its great, round, red eyes then bad luck or even death will swiftly follow. At other times, Shuck brings rather better luck. One man in Lincolnshire encountered Shuck when walking home from the pub and came to a stop in understandable alarm – thus saving himself from being involved in a nasty road crash as a car mounted the pavement just where he would have been if he had not stopped.

The Seven Hills Road, north of Cobham and close to the junction with Chestnut Avenue, where several motorists have sighted an enigmatic old lady.

West Street in Farnham is a busy thoroughfare during the day, but at evening it is quieter and that is when the old lady phantom is most often seen about.

The Old Guildford Road runs south-east out of Frimley to Pirbright Common, where it becomes a track, then peters out as a bridleway running over the common toward Guildford – the more modern surfaced road takes a more northerly track.

One person about whom a great deal is known is Field Marshal Lord Ligonier, who haunts the lanes north of Downside, close to his old home of Cobham Park. Born into rather modest circumstances in 1680, he joined the Army in 1702 and rose rapidly through the ranks by a combination of luck, hard work and outstanding bravery. By 1720, he was colonel of the 7th Dragoon Guards, which he made one of the finest cavalry regiments in Europe. He was promoted to be a general in 1735 and served with distinction until 1747, when he was badly wounded and captured by the French at the Battle of Val. After being released he held a series of high-ranking posts in both the military and government but did not again go to war. He was made an earl on his retirement, when he went to live at Cobham Park.

It was not Ligonier's heroic military career that ensured his fame in Surrey so much as his scandalous private life. Throughout his time in the Army, Ligonier had maintained that his career was more important to him than marriage. He indulged in a number of affairs, sometimes with married women, but did not marry. On his retirement some expected him finally to marry, but instead he nominated his nephew as the heir to his wealth, estates and titles and set off on a determinedly debauched lifestyle.

The villagers of Downside were treated to the sight of Ligonier, now aged in his sixties, throwing wild parties for his old military cronies and new-found friends from London. The parties were notorious for their heavy drinking and lewd behaviour, but that was not the end of it. Ligonier also took fairly seriously his habit of seducing local farm girls. Unlike the typical wicked squire of English legend, Ligonier did not cruelly cast off the girls when he had tired

The Black Dog of Farnham is a monstrous hound that has much in common with other supernatural dogs reported elsewhere in England.

of them. Instead he gave the young women comfortable rooms at Cobham Park and ensured that the illegitimate children were given a sound education. The sons were given introductions to Ligonier's friends who could get them started on a career in the Army, law or some other respectable profession. The daughters were given dowries handsome enough to make them good catches for local farmers, despite their illegitimate birth. All in all, he looked after his collection of mistresses and bastards rather well. At the time of his death there were a dozen women living with him at Cobham Park.

His ghost first appeared very soon after his death. It was seen walking the lanes dressed in an old Army greatcoat and walking with stately tread and straight back – just as Ligonier had been in the habit of doing when out for a stroll. Unfortunately the ghost does not seem to have appeared since the 1960s. Perhaps the conversion of his old home into a luxury apartment block has rather put him off returning to Downside.

Considerably less fortunate than Ligonier was Christopher Slaughterford, who failed to live to an old age due to his execution for a murder that many people thought he did not commit. Slaughterford was the son of a miller who set up as a malster in Shalford and by the age of thirty had acquired a considerable fortune. He was courting a Shalford girl by the name of Jane Young, who was considered one of the prettiest, but poorest, girls in the neighbourhood.

Cobham Park has now been converted into a number of prestigious apartments, but it was originally built as a comfortable country home for Field Marshal Lord Ligonier after he retired from the Army in the mid-eighteenth century. His ghost still wanders the lanes near his old home.

On the evening of 5 October 1703, Jane left her parent's home to go walking with Slaughterford. She never came home again. Slaughterford claimed that he had left her around 9 p.m. within sight of her home and gone straight home. However, it was noticed that he did not seem to be unduly worried about his missing fiancée. At one point he even said that if he ever got married he would make sure that his bride had a good dowry. Suspicions grew.

Six weeks later, Jane's body was found hidden on farmland. She seemed to have been strangled. The local magistrates began an investigation, and Slaughterford was soon arrested. There was no firm evidence against him. However, it was thought that he may have murdered Jane in order to get rid of her if he were truly intent on marrying a rich bride. He was sent to the Marshalsea Prison in London while investigations were carried out. At a hearing in Kingston upon Thames, a jury decided that Jane Young had been murdered, but that there was not enough evidence to name Slaughterford or anyone else as the guilty man.

The villagers in Shalford were unimpressed. Jane's father was convinced that his daughter had been murdered by her lover. Because the Young family were so poor, a public collection was got up and soon enough money had been subscribed to bring a private prosecution against Slaughterford. At the trial a great deal of circumstantial evidence was given. Jane's employer, Mrs Chapman, testified that Jane had handed in her notice a couple of days before she disappeared, stating that she was about to get married to Slaughterford. Mrs Chapman said that the girl had shown her the wedding dress she had bought. The dress was nowhere to be found after the girl vanished.

A waggoner was found who had been driving a transport wagon from Guildford to Horsham on the night that Jane went missing. He said that sometime past midnight he had been passing through Shalford and had seen a young woman walking along the road arm in arm with a young man. The descriptions he gave were rather vague, but they did match Jane and Slaughterford up to a point. Slaughterford, it will be recalled, had said he went home to bed at about 9 p.m.

By the standards of the time, the evidence against Slaughterford was weak, and yet the Guildford jury found him guilty of murder and he was hanged on 9 July. Even as he stood in the shadow of the scaffold, Slaughterford declared his innocence. It was widely thought at the time that the guilty verdict was due not so much to the evidence presented in court as to the strong feeling in the area against Slaughterford.

Within a few weeks of the execution it began to be whispered that Slaughterford was not resting in his grave. His phantom had been seen stalking the lanes around Shalford. According to the more lurid accounts, the ghost appeared with the hangman's rope dangling from his neck, carrying a burning torch in his hand and repeatedly screaming the single word 'Vengeance!' His ghost has been seen right up to the present day, though more modern accounts describe the phantom as being silent and carrying a lantern or lamp.

Not far south of Shalford lies Bramley, and east of that village the road to Wonersh climbs up over Chinthurst Hill. It is along this road, Chinthurst Lane, that an old horse-drawn caravan has been seen driven by an elderly woman. She is generally identified as being a gypsy from the nineteenth century, though why she haunts this area is unknown.

Equally anonymous is the man seen on Carthouse Lane, Horsell. He stomps along with a rucksack on his back, but nobody seems to know why. The phantom woman who walks along the southern end of Hayes Lane, Kenley, carries in her arms a young child. She is sometimes

The ghost of Horsell's Carthouse Lane walks with a steady tramp and a rucksack over his shoulder – but where he is going and why he walks is utterly unknown.

said to be a nun, though there seems to be no evidence for this. Also seen in Hayes Lane is a man in what seems to be fashions dating from the 1930s. He is sighted most often on the bridge right at the northern end of the lane, beside the railway station. He is generally thought to be waiting for a train – either to take him away or perhaps one that is bringing a particular person to him.

A road of a rather special kind is haunted by the very persistent spectre of Percy Lambert. The road in question is the roadway of the Brooklands Race Track, south-west of Weybridge. The track is now incomplete, being abandoned in the 1940s as motor racing developed beyond the limitations of the facilities at Brooklands. Today the former racetrack is home to shops, an industrial estate and a fine transport museum.

The race track was built in 1907 as a three mile oval of concrete track, 100ft wide and with a special starting straight down the middle. The huge corners at either end of the track were steeply banked to help the drivers stay on the course when travelling at speed. At this date, motor racing was in its infancy and was organised by the Jockey Club, which ran the horse racing season. Even the drivers wore coloured outfits for identification like jockeys – the numbering of cars did not become common until the increasing speeds meant that spectators did not get a chance to see the coloured shirts.

One of the greatest drivers of these early years was Percy Lambert. In February 1913 he became the first man to drive at over 100mph. The record did not last long for a Frenchman, Jean Chassagne, topped 107mph in June. Lambert was keen to regain the speed record for himself and for Britain. His sponsor, the Earl of Shrewsbury, put up the money to enable the Talbot Motor Company to produce a unique, streamlined version of their racing car and to fit it with a specially prepared 4,754cc engine. On 31 October 1913, Percy Lambert came to Brooklands to regain the record.

After final checks to ensure that the car was in perfect condition, Lambert fired up the engine and set off at 9.20 a.m. The car was running perfectly and was soon thundering round the course, averaging 110.4mph. Then as the car entered the northern embanked corner, there was a bang.

'He has burst a tyre,' declared Major Lloyd, the clerk of the course. He was right, the nearside rear tyre had blown out. The car swerved at high speed down the embankment, regained a straight course as the brakes were applied, then span sideways, flipped over and began rolling over and over. Lambert was thrown clear to skid along the concrete road surface. The spectators went running to the stricken man even before the car had crashed to a halt. He was lifted gently into an awaiting ambulance and rushed to hospital, but in vain. He died later that day.

The steeply banked corners of Brooklands Race Track now stand empty and overgrown, but in the early years of the twentieth century they were the centrepiece of the greatest and most modern motor racing track in the world. Today, they are haunted by the ghost of a racing driver who was fatally injured here when his car crashed.

The old pit buildings have largely been removed at Brooklands as the site has been redeveloped. However, these structures remain on what was once the long finishing straight.

But Percy Lambert has not left Brooklands, at least not if the stories are to be believed. Dressed in tight leather overalls with a leather helmet and goggles, his ghost has been seen on and off over the years. Several night watchmen at the industrial estate, and the Vickers aircraft factory that preceded it, have reported seeing the enigmatic figure wandering around the place after dark. In 1973 one such worker reported hearing the sounds of a car crash, complete with skidding tyres and rending metal. He ran to investigate, only to find the old racetrack totally empty. Only when his report was compared with old records did it emerge that the sounds had come from the site of the Lambert crash.

The ghost of Lambert walks Brooklands still – just as so many other highways and byways around Surrey still play host to their ghosts.

FOUR

PUB PHANTOMS

There are many fine pubs, inns and restaurants in Surrey. It seems that the folk of the county enjoy eating out and meeting each other for a drink as much as anyone else. There seems no logical reason why the ghosts of the county should not likewise enjoy a trip to the local. Indeed, it sometimes seems as if the hostelries might be almost as busy with their spectral customers as with the humans.

Even so, two ghosts in one building might seem a bit excessive, but the Marquis of Granby manages to cope. The pub lies beside the A307, at the roundabout known locally as the Scilly Isles. The modern extensions to this pub hide the fact that it dates back almost 400 years, and it is in the oldest part of the pub that the ghost – or ghosts – lurk.

Mark Nicholls, a former bar manager, talked about the haunting in 2002:

> The lady upstairs. We all know her. I've only heard her once myself, but everyone knows all about her. You hear her footsteps behind you and some rustling – like a silk dress they tell me. Then when you turn around there is nobody there. It's a really weird feeling to know that somebody is in the room with you, but there isn't really. Mind you, she's no bother really. It gives you a bit of a start, that's all.

Nobody seems to know who this ghost is, though she is usually described as a servant girl. From the descriptions given by those who have heard the footsteps and skirts of the ghostly lady, she would seem to date back at least 180 years. The dainty steps and heavy silk rustling seem to indicate fashions from the early nineteenth century at least. And stories of the ghost have been circulating in the area since the late nineteenth century when a local gentleman mentioned the story as typical of the gullible nature of local farming folk.

But the ghostly goings-on at the Marquis of Granby are not entirely harmless. In one of the upstairs rooms is a small cupboard set into a wall. The door is nailed shut and an old Bible is kept pushed against it. A former employee at the pub said that the Bible must never be moved or 'the thing in the cupboard' will get out. This 'thing' was a most dreadful phantom much given to slamming doors, smashing crockery and hammering on the walls. It made life a misery at the Marquis in the middle of the nineteenth century. However, all that is of the past since a passing clergyman banished the 'thing' to the cupboard and left his Bible to secure the door with holy powers.

The Marquis of Granby stands on the old Porstmouth Road a mile or so east of Esher. It is reputed to have been haunted by two phantoms, though only the gentler of the two still walks the building.

But the lady continues to walk. Not that she is much trouble, of course. So long as she does not learn how to open a particular cupboard door, that is.

Another serving girl haunts the Oatlands Park Hotel in Weybridge. She is said to date back to the time when this was a private home of grand proportions. For some unknown reason she had a blazing row with her boyfriend. After the argument, she arrived back at the servants' quarters in tears, stammered out an incoherent account of the confrontation, then ran upstairs and threw herself out of a window to her death. She is said to be seen most often in and around the restaurant. The Selsdon Park Hotel in Croydon also has a ghostly presence that is said to be that of a serving girl who committed suicide. This phantom is seen walking along the Tudor Corridor carrying a lit candle in her hands.

Also the phantom of a servant is the lady in grey who frequents the Lion & Lamb in Farnham. This particular phantom is said to wear a large hat with a wide brim as she walks across the courtyard. She is rather irregular in her habits. The manageress during the 1970s reported that the ghost might be seen several times in one week, then not turn up again for months. The reason why she is identified as a maid is that footsteps and swishing skirts are heard pottering about the rooms. It is usually assumed the two phantoms are one and the same, though they may not be.

Also in Farnham is the Hop Bag Inn, where the courtyard is haunted by a ghostly coach. The vehicle, pulled by a pair of horses, comes trotting into the yard and then vanishes. It is sometimes accompanied by the phantom of a young woman with a mournful expression on her face.

Weybridge's Oatlands Park Hotel was originally a private house, and the gentle phantom seen here dates back to those early days.

Rather more cheerful is the jovial spectre at the fifteenth-century Grantley Arms in Wonersh. This phantom was formerly seen during the Christmas season and was most often encountered in the bar area where he was apparently laughing at some joke told by an invisible companion. For some reason he was said to be a monk – perhaps he wore some sort of gown or habit. In any case, he does not seem to have been seen in recent years. The identification of the ghost as a monk has some credibility as the building was originally erected as a monastic hospice.

A similarly vague phantom was the figure in white seen at the Castle restaurant in Sunbury-on-Thames. None of those who have seen it are able to say if it is a boy or a girl, only that it flits about in the kitchen and adjacent areas. Just as enigmatic is the ghost at the Angel in Sutton. Some say it is a boy, others a fully grown man. The ghost at the White Hart in Pirbright, meanwhile, is best known for its large black hat. Most witnesses comment on the hat, but seem unable to describe the ghostly figure wearing it in any real detail.

The King's Head in Chertsey has a ghostly monk or priest. He has been seen quite clearly several times over the years by a number of different witness. Mostly he seems content to potter about the ancient building on whatever business brings him here. He managed to get himself into the press on one dramatic occasion. An Australian barmaid was sleeping upstairs in 1977 when she woke up in the middle of the night to find her bedclothes in a heap on the floor and the phantom monk standing in her room, apparently watching her carefully. The startled girl fled and refused to go back into the building ever again.

Another monk is linked to the haunting at the Golden Grove, also in Chertsey. The ghost here is that of a young woman in a long, grey dress. The legend usually told about her is that

The Grantley Arms at Wonersh is home to a spectre who only appears in the run up to Christmas.

she was a serving girl at the inn who was seduced by a heartless monk or clergyman. When the girl fell pregnant her cruel lover either murdered her, or spurned her and so caused her suicide. Either way, the poor young woman died and now returns in phantom fashion.

Yet another tavern in Chertsey, the Old Mitre Inn, is also haunted. The ghost here is said to be that of a soldier dressed in the fine red coat worn by soldiers in the nineteenth century. He is seen most often near the front door. A second phantom is that of a young woman who wears clothes that seem to date from the same era as the soldier. Presumably the two are linked in some way, but nobody seems to know how.

Guildford's Angel Hotel has a ghostly Army officer stalking its rooms. The ghost was first noticed in the 1960s, at least so far as the written record is concerned. In 1970, a couple staying in Room 1, a Mr and Mrs Dell, saw the phantom. Mr Dell was something of an artist so he quickly sketched the figure that he and his wife had seen. The ghost was clearly wearing an old-fashioned Army uniform, perhaps of Boer War vintage.

During the 1980s the Crown Inn at Oxted was troubled by a number of mysterious 'cold spots', as they were termed by the then landlord, Dennis Cornish. Certain rooms or areas of the pub would feel cold and chilly for a few minutes, or sometimes hours, before returning to normal. After putting up with this for some time, Cornish one day saw a woman in an old-fashioned dress walking along an upstairs landing. As the startled publican watched, the figure simply faded away in front of his eyes.

Cornish summoned a spiritualist, who visited the pub. He wandered about for some time before declaring that one of the upstairs rooms – which had suffered especially from cold spots

The ghost at Chertsey's town centre pub, the King's Head, so terrified a barmaid that she fled and refused to ever return.

The gentle phantom to be found at the Golden Grove near Chertsey has a sad and tragic history behind her.

– held the source of the trouble. The spiritualist said that he could sense a woman who was very angry with her husband. He went on to describe the woman, who seemed to be almost identical to the spectral figure Cornish had seen on the landing outside the room.

Cornish then set about researching the history of the pub. He found that during the 1930s, the pub had been run by a Canadian, Pierre La Mont, and his English wife, Charlotte. In 1938, Charlotte threw out her husband, who had acquired a reputation as a drunk and who, she alleged, was boozing and gambling his way through the profits of the inn. Charlotte herself had given up the pub in 1939, apparently moving to South Africa. There had been no tragic death involved, but at least the description of an angry woman in 1930s fashion did match Mrs La Mont.

A tragic death does lie behind the haunting of Ockley's Red Lion. Back in the nineteenth century, a lady was thrown from her horse nearby and brought here to recover. The injuries did not seem very serious, but she died within a few hours. Her ghost, clad in riding cloak and boots, still walks the pub.

In Purley, the Royal Oak is haunted by a genial old boy who is seen pottering around in the lounge bar. He is sometimes, but not always, said to have a walking stick. Either way he does not seem to hang about, as he is rarely seen for more than a second or two. A similarly kindly old man haunts the Sandrock pub in Croydon. This phantom has a long, grey beard and wears a black suit that some think means he must have been a priest or vicar when alive.

Lingfield's Greyhound Inn is said to be haunted by the ghost of a young boy, aged around eight or so. Who he might be is quite unknown, but he is blamed for various ghostly childish pranks such as lights being flicked off when they should be on and small objects going missing. The pub was formerly famous for a rather different paranormal reason. There used to be a pond outside in the days before the internal combustion engine replaced horses on the roads of England. For some unaccountable reason, passing horses, whether ridden or pulling coaches and carts, often felt an irresistible urge to walk into the pond and then stand there. It always took a great effort to get the errant horses to leave the pond.

Godalming's King's Arms has a somewhat unusual ghost. It is never seen, but is heard very often. When people are in the bar they will hear the sound of a man in heavy boots walking into a bedroom upstairs. The footsteps then stop as if the man has sat down, after which comes the heavy thump-thump of the boots being taken off and dropped onto the floor. Then there is silence.

The King's Arms in central Godalming is a large and welcoming old coaching inn. The phantom here is unusual in that it is often heard, but never seen.

FIVE

OTHER GHOSTS

Although Surrey has more than its fair share of haunted pubs and highways, many other spooks and spectres can be found in a wide range of places. Some are in houses, others in factories, several in churches and not a few simply pottering about the countryside.

One of the best known of the Surrey ghosts is the White Lady of Farnham. This particular phantom is said to haunt the church, or more particularly the tower. She has been seen many times by locals as they stroll past the church. The White Lady usually behaves in much the same way. She stands on top of the tower, leaning over the battlements and peering down on the town. One witness claims to have seen her clamber up onto the parapet and hurl herself off to fall, screaming, toward the flagstones far below.

Other churches in Surrey are also haunted. That at Limpsfield is home to the ghost of a homeless child who died a sad and neglected death some centuries ago. Bletchington Church has a spectral woman flitting about the churchyard. She is said to be dressed in fashions of the seventeenth century, but most of the descriptions are fairly vague. Cobham's St Andrew's Church has a most peculiar ghost in the churchyard – that of a donkey. The church at Leatherhead is home to a ghostly man dressed in a long brown habit, so he is usually identified as being a monk. Reigate's St Mary's Church has an apparently happy phantom. The ghost is that of a young girl who skips and dances up the main path.

The ruins of Waverley Abbey, which lie in the meadows south of Waverley Lane and to the south-east of Farnham, are said to be haunted by a monk. This phantom cleric strides slowly but purposefully among the ruins with his head bowed as if he is searching for something on the ground. Local legend has it that this is the ghost of a monk who bravely defied the agents of King Henry VIII when they came to close down the abbey during the Reformation. Believing that God was on his side, the monk barred entrance to the abbey to the King's men. The Royal men then sent for a gang of soldiers, who grabbed the monk and strung him up from the nearest tree.

There is, in fact, no evidence that any of the monks at Waverley resisted the closure of their abbey, still less that one of them was murdered for his actions. There were a few executions during the Dissolution of the Monasteries, but these always followed trials and concerned men who disputed the King's right to be head of the Church of England rather than those who simply got in the way of the agents. In fact, the monks and nuns turfed out of their religious houses were given pensions on which to live and not a few subsequently rejoined the Church of England in one capacity or another. Which leaves open the question of why the monk at Waverley cannot find rest five centuries after his death.

An ecclesiastical ghost of rather more certain identity is Bishop Lancelot Andrewes, who haunts the old rectory and church at Cheam. Born at Barking and educated at Cambridge, Andrewes entered the church in 1580 at the age of twenty-five. He became the vicar at Cheam and resided here for many years. His powerful preaching and impressive oratory brought him to the notice of Queen Elizabeth I and then King James I, who asked him to join the team producing the translation of the Bible into English that would become known as the King James Bible. In 1605, he was promoted to be Bishop of Chichester, then further promoted to Winchester in 1609.

Cobham's St Andrew's Church has what is probably the most unusual ghost wandering around the churchyard – that of a donkey.

Although Waverley Abbey is best known for its links to Sir Walter Scott's novel of the same name, in its day it was better known for piety and learning. Today the ruins are open to the public free of charge and are an attractive place to visit – so long as the ghost does not make an appearance.

The quiet ruins of Waverley Abbey are haunted by a phantom monk who walks with his head bent forwards as if searching the ground for something – but what he never tells.

King Henry VIII, who gave the orders to close down Waverley Abbey and so set in train the sequence of events that would lead to the haunting that has lasted to the present day.

The ghost of the great Elizabethan adventurer and courtier Sir Walter Raleigh haunts the church at West Horsley – or rather, a part of him does.

It would seem that he was happiest in Cheam, however. Soon after his death in 1618, his ghost began to be seen here. It walks still, though apparently not as frequently as it once did.

The ghost of another famous Elizabethan, Sir Walter Raleigh, haunts the church at West Horsley. Raleigh led an adventurous life as a seaman, courtier and soldier. He raided Spanish ships, fought Irish rebels and tried to establish English colonies in North America. Despite these and many other achievements, he is best known for two notable facts. The first is that one day when Queen Elizabeth was out walking at Richmond she came to a muddy puddle in the path. While the other courtiers were debating what to do, Raleigh whipped off his cloak and laid it in the mud so that the Queen could cross without getting her feet dirty. The second is that he brought potatoes and tobacco back from the Americas, being the first person to introduce either to Britain. By 1618 the new ruler, James I, wanted to make peace with Spain. The Spanish demanded the execution of Raleigh as part of the peace deal, so James sent him to the scaffold. Raleigh's head was spiked on London Bridge for a while, but later his son, Carew, was allowed to take it away for burial near his home in West Horsley. Although it is said to be Raleigh's ghost which is seen at West Horsley churchyard, it takes a very unusual form. The spectral head alone is seen, hovering over the spot where it lies buried.

It is said that the ghost of a king haunts Farnham Library. The library is housed in what was once Vernon House and the ill-fated monarch, King Charles I, stayed here after his arrest on the orders of Parliament and before his trial and execution in London. The ghost of a man on the stairs and landing could, from the descriptions given of it, be almost any man in a tall-crowned hat and short coat. As for the smell of violets that unaccountably fills some rooms, it need not necessarily come from Charles, although he is known to have used a scent of that nature.

Just west of Godalming Station stands Westbrook Place. In the eighteenth century, this was home to the Oglethorpe family. The family was an important one, providing colonial governors and government ministers to the service of the nation. They did, however, hide a secret, for the Oglethorpe's were of the opinion that King James II had been ousted illegally from the throne of Britain. While King George of Hanover was widely accepted as King of Britain, the Oglethorpes thought that Prince Charles Edward Stuart, grandson of James II, had a better claim to be King.

When Prince Charles, better known to history as Bonnie Prince Charlie, tried to claim his throne in the 1745 Jacobite Rebellion, the Oglethorpes prepared to rise and join him. The Scottish rebels got no further south than Derby, however, and the Oglethorpes stayed at home. Some twenty years later they got exciting news. Bonnie Prince Charlie was coming to Britain once again. This time he was not coming with sword in hand, but disguised as a perfectly respectable Italian count. The Prince asked if he could stay at Westbrook for a few days, and the Oglethorpes agreed with delight.

Farnham Library is housed in what was Vernon House, one of the most prestigious houses in the town during the seventeenth century. The ghost here is rumoured to be that of King Charles I.

Godalming's Westbrook Place is now home to a medical trust, but in its day was one of the most prestigious houses in Surrey. The ghost here is of a political exile who paid an incognito visit to England that might have cost him his life.

King Charles I, whose ghost is said to walk Farnham Library, was held a prisoner here overnight on his way to London to stand trial for alleged treason against the people of England.

The death warrant of King Charles I was signed by the men who tried him. With the production of this warrant, it became clear that the King's night in Farnham had been the last that he would spend outside his prison in London.

So it was that a tall, handsome foreigner came to Godalming. The locals had all been primed with the story that he was an Italian nobleman and treated him with due respect when he went into town. He stayed for a few weeks, then left. His true identity was not revealed until many years later, when it was no longer politically dangerous to have been on friendly terms with the Prince. It is said that the tall man in a grey cloak who walks the grounds of Westbrook is none other than Bonnie Prince Charlie. He has been seen walking along Westbrook Road and down to the River Wey, as well as in the gardens of the house.

Loseley House is a fine Elizabethan mansion that is still inhabited by the descendants of its builders. The current Mr and Mrs More-Molyneux open the house to the public, but also continue to run the estate as a farming business. They are best known for the Loseley ice creams and yoghurts which can be found in many Surrey shops. There are said to be two phantoms here, both of them ladies dating from the eighteenth century. Although the two ghosts look similar, they are very different entities. One goes by the name of the Pleasant Lady, the other is known as the Unpleasant Lady.

The different names are prompted by the emotions that the two ghosts inspire in those that encounter them. The Pleasant Lady emits an aura of charm and friendliness. Those unfortunate enough to meet the Unpleasant Lady report that when she appears, the room is filled with a feeling of hostility and hatred that can be astonishingly intense. One American visitor who met her in the 1930s fled not only the room, but also the house. He refused to re-enter and waited outside while somebody else did his packing for him. Then he left.

Off the B2128 east of Cranleigh lies Baynards Park, a charming Tudor mansion that was – and some think still is – home to Sir Thomas More. More was born into a good family in 1478 and was well educated. He trained as a lawyer, but was soon employed by the government of Henry VII. Under Henry VIII, he became Speaker of the House of Commons, then occupied a number of ministerial posts. In 1529, he was raised to the position of Lord Chancellor, then the highest ministerial position in government, but soon he fell out with the King's religious policies and resigned.

Over the years that followed, More became a rallying point for others opposed to Henry VIII's policies. In 1535, Henry decided to make an example of More. He demanded that More recognise that the King, not the Pope, was head of the Church of England. More refused, so Henry had him executed. The severed head was put on a spike over the gate of the City of London that faced onto London Bridge. More's daughter, Margaret, bribed the gatekeeper to throw the head into the Thames as she was passing under the bridge in a boat rowed by an accomplice. She then brought the head back to Baynards Place for burial.

The phantom of Sir Thomas More is said to haunt the grounds around Baynards Park. Presumably he is looking for his lost head.

Tadworth Court, near Banstead, is now a hospital for children, though it was originally built as a private home and it is to those early days that the origins of the haunting belong.

On the stairs of the house there is a portrait of a young woman sitting in a lush landscape. She is dressed in a long white dress with red bows on the bodice and shoulders. Peering out from behind a tree over the woman's left shoulder is another face, one that does not seem to fit the composition of the portrait and one which, moreover, has a sinister expression on its face.

According to a local legend, the portrait is that of a daughter of the house who lived here with her family and younger sister in the reign of King George I. The young woman fell in love with a wealthy young man from Epsom and a marriage was soon in the offing. The portrait was

The great Tudor statesman and saint, Sir Thomas More, haunts Baynards Park just outside Cranleigh. This portrait by Hans Holbein was painted when he was still in favour with King Henry VIII and a key figure in Royal government. He would later retire to Baynards Park after quarrelling with the King, but this did not save him from execution.

painted to celebrate the happy news and hung in the house. Unknown to the girl, however, her sister loved the same man and was becoming unhinged by jealousy.

One day the young gentleman from Epsom came calling. He entered the front door and his voice echoed up the stairs. His fiancée came out on to the landing to greet him and leaned over the balustrade. The looks of love that passed between them was too much for the younger sister. She threw herself at her sister and hurled her over the balustrade to fall to her death on the tiled floor far below. The distraught girl then ran up to the roof and jumped to her death.

The family sorrowfully arranged for the funeral of the two girls at the local church. When they came back from the service, they were horrified to see that the face of the younger daughter had mysteriously appeared in the portrait of her sister. The family at once moved the painting to the attic, but that prompted the start of the hauntings. The phantoms of the two girls came back to recreate the fatal series of events, complete with heart-rending screams. It was too much and the portrait was returned to the staircase, where it remains.

Unfortunately for the legend, the records show no such event ever took place at Tadworth Court. It seems that the story was invented to explain the rather curious portrait.

Standing in the centre of Thames Ditton is a large brick house built in 1786 for the Walsingham family as Boyle House, but now known as the Home of Compassion, as it is owned by the Church of England Community of the Compassion of Christ. The house passed to Lady Charlotte Walsingham and her husband, Lord Henry Fitzgerald. His brother, Edward, was shot dead as a rebel during the 1798 uprising in Ireland led by Wolfe Tone. His widow, a beautiful young French woman named Pamela, came to live in Boyle House. Her life was further blighted by tragedy when her father was guillotined by the new French republican government. La Bella Pamela, as the lady was known, proved to be restless. She journeyed widely through Europe, but always came back to Thames Ditton.

She eventually died in Paris and was a buried in Montmartre. But her travels were not yet over. In 1870, her tomb was destroyed by a Prussian artillery shell. Her bones were collected up, and later brought to Thames Ditton where they were reburied in the church. It is said that the lone female figure who walks the corridors and rooms of the Home of Compassion is the phantom of La Bella Pamela, finally come home to Thames Ditton for good.

Not all of Surrey's ghosts inhabit grand houses. The phantom of a teenage girl in Victorian dress haunts a shop in Bramley High Street. A rather similar young woman haunts a house in Carshalton, while a third teenage girl is often encountered in a house on Godstone Road, Caterham. A teenage boy in a modern-looking jumper haunts the garden of a house in Addiscombe.

One haunted house in Surrey made legal history in 1904 when it became the centre of a protracted legal battle that rumbled on until 1907. The house in question was Hillside, a grand Victorian villa on Egham Hill in Egham. According to local legend, the building was haunted by the phantom of a fairly short, muscular man. This was said to be the ghost of a farmer who had murdered a child in the old farmhouse that had occupied the site before Hillside was built.

The story, complete with lurid but anonymous accounts of sightings by former inhabitants and their staff, appeared in the *Daily Mail* and the *Daily Express*. The owner of the house took legal action against the newspapers, alleging that the stories had made the house virtually worthless as he could not find any tenants willing to rent it. The newspapers tried to argue that ghosts did not exist and so there was no case to answer, even though the stories they had run had argued persuasively that ghosts were indeed there. The judge clamped down on that. He ruled that the case did not revolve around whether or not ghosts existed, but whether or not the stories had affected the value of the property. Evidence was produced to prove that they had, whereupon the newspapers changed their defence to one of fair reporting. They said that everyone in the Egham area knew all about the ghost and that all they had been doing was passing on well established facts – thus contradicting their earlier suggestion that ghosts did not exist. In the end, the case was settled by the payment of damages.

The villa is still there, now converted into apartments. There has been no news on the ghost for some decades; presumably he has gone.

The church at Thames Ditton holds the grave of Lady Fitzgerald, better known as La Bella Pamela, one of the great society beauties of the early nineteenth century. She led a tragic life and returns to the village in spectral form.

SIX

BIZARRE STORIES

Surrey has some strange stories to tell, but none more weird than that of the Godalming woman who apparently gave birth to rabbits.

This odd story begins in November 1726 when Mrs Mary Tofts reached the final stages of her fourth pregnancy. Mary was the wife of a weaver in Godalming and had spent her twenty-five or so years in respectable, if somewhat impoverished, obscurity. Everything changed in hours.

John Howard, an unqualified doctor from Guildford, attended the birth. He emerged from the Tofts' household brandishing a litter of rabbits which, he said, had been produced instead of a baby. Word of the amazing birth spread rapidly and the local gentry flocked to Godalming to see the rabbits and talk to Mary Tofts. Naturally, a few pence were paid to Dr Howard on each visit.

Mary Tofts told all her eager visitors about her odd pregnancy. She told how she had been startled by a large rabbit leaping from a hedge in the very earliest days of the pregnancy and of how she had developed insatiable cravings for rabbit meat in the later stages and of her bizarre dreams about rabbits. All very odd.

When word reached London, the more firebrand clergy saw the culmination of an obscure Biblical prophecy in the birth. Ladies at Court became worried that they might be affected by the expected epidemic of animal births. King George I's personal anatomist, Nathaniel St André, was sent to Godalming to investigate. When he arrived more money, naturally, changed hands.

While St André was in Godalming, Mary Tofts suddenly went in to labour. St André hurried from his lodgings to the Tofts' house and arrived just in time to see what appeared to be Mary giving birth to two live rabbits. St André was convinced and reported back to the King that miraculous animal births were, indeed, taking place in Godalming.

Queen Caroline, however, was not convinced. She objected to the state of terror affecting the ladies at Court and determined to settle matters. She sent for Mary Tofts and John Howard and installed them in rooms in West London where the Royal gynaecologist, Sir Richard Manningham, could keep a close eye on the woman.

A few days later, Mary Tofts gave birth again. This time no live rabbits emerged, but instead pieces of a dead rabbit came forth. Manningham was not fooled. He had seen Howard slip something beneath the bed sheets and believed them to be the rabbit joints. The case was clinched when a local butcher revealed he had been paid a large sum of money for a rabbit on condition of utmost secrecy on the day of the 'birth'. He identified the purchaser as Howard.

Although Howard denied any fraud and insisted on the truth of the rabbit births, Mary Tofts broke down and confessed. Both she and Howard spent time in prison for cheating people of the money they had paid to see the Rabbit Woman and her brood. Then both returned home and picked up their lives where they had left off. Only the anatomist, St André, suffered in the long term. His credulity led to his reputation being ruined. His career over, he left Court and returned to Germany in obscurity.

The career of the Rabbit Woman of Godalming was over, but her fame lived on. Even eighty years later, a traveller to Guildford heard locals call men from Godalming 'rabbits' – behind their backs at least.

Although most modern investigators write the entire episode off as a fraud from start to finish, those who were there at the time did not. Undoubtedly the later incidents were fakery perpetrated in the hope of earning money, but there were plenty of people in Godalming who were convinced that Mary Tofts really had given birth to rabbits. It was not until the 1930s that a possible solution to the enigma occurred. A woman in northern England gave birth to many very small, underdeveloped embryos – almost twenty of them. It was considered a freak event where she had produced a lot of eggs all at once, which had all been fertilized and grown to a certain size, until there was no room for them and they were expelled. Of course, they all died. To a poorly educated country woman of the eighteenth century, the poorly-formed embryos might have more resembled rabbit young than they did human babies. If this is what happened, then one must assume that Howard saw a way of making money out of the unusual event, after which events spiralled out of control once the Court took an interest.

If the bizarre births at Godalming were related to life's beginning, other bizarre happenings in Surrey were concerned with its ending. The most prominent of these concerns Major Peter Labelliere, a retired Army officer, of Dorking. Labelliere was commissioned into the Army as a lieutenant on 17 January 1760 and seems to have led a perfectly straightforward, if rather unspectacular, career. He retired as a major sometime in the 1780s and proposed marriage to a young lady named Hetty Fletcher. She rejected him in harsh and rather heartless terms, the details of which were not recorded. After this rejection, the major began to show signs of mental instability.

By the 1790s, Labelliere had become a noted character of Dorking. He lived in a modest house in South Street, in the town centre, rented from the woman who lived next door with her family. He attended church regularly and piously and was always generous in giving alms to the poor. He was particularly kindly to children. He pottered around the town quite genially and was generally well liked. Unfortunately he did not wash often, if at all, and smelled badly on most occasions.

His favourite pastime was writing on religion and politics. He was a frequent correspondent with the newspapers, both locally and in London, taking issue with speeches made by ministers or with sermons preached by clergy. He wrote numerous pamphlets, mostly on religious matters, which he paid to have published in London and handed out to whoever would take them. He was frequently seen walking about with newspapers and other papers bulging from his pockets while he scribbled in a notebook. His opinions and views were generally well argued, but ultimately nonsensical and often inconsistent.

On one matter he never varied his opinion. He was going to die in the year 1800 – a prediction that he told to all his acquaintances. When the fatal year finally arrived, Major Labelliere added an extra detail. His death would occur on 1 June. No doubt about it, he said. Nobody took him very seriously; after all, he was not quite right in the head and seemed in robust health.

On 31 May he went around Dorking to say goodbye to his friends, wrote a string of letters to acquaintances outside the town and left detailed instructions for his burial. Next morning, he went next door to bid farewell to his landlady and her two young children. Then he went back home, sat down in his favourite armchair and died.

The instructions for his funeral were carried out to the letter on 4 June. Word had leaked out that these were rather bizarre and the whole town turned out to watch. His body was put into a coffin together with mementoes of his military career and a conventional funeral service was performed at the church. The coffin was then loaded onto a cart and carried up to the summit of Box Hill, which towers over the town two miles to the north-east. A hole had already been dug on the hill that was 3ft square and 12ft deep.

Once the coffin was unloaded from the cart, a band struck up a lively dance tune. The landlady's two children were then led forward and asked to dance on the coffin, as Labelliere had requested. The little girl burst into tears and only sat on the coffin, but the boy stepped up and danced a lively jig while the band played on. The coffin was then lowered carefully into the hole head first. Chalk rubble was packed around the box to hold it securely vertical, then the hole was filled in with chalk and soil. A monument was later erected a few feet from the grave, the precise site of which is now open to debate.

The reason for the bizarre burial is not entirely clear. We know that Labelliere wanted dancing at his funeral to show that a death was not a cause for sorrow but joy, as it meant the soul of the deceased was free to go to join God and Christ in Heaven. Most locals believed that Labelliere wanted to be buried upside down due to the fact that he thought the world

The view from Box Hill over the town of Dorking. It was this view that Major Peter Labelliere wanted to enjoy for all eternity, an ambition that was to lead to a most bizarre funeral.

had turned topsy-turvy and that being buried in this way would mean that he alone was the right way up. Those who had read his rambling religious tracts, however, suggested that he was imitating St Peter, who had asked to be crucified hanging upside down as he was not fit to die in the same manner as Christ. In other words, he was showing his humility before God.

We may never know the truth about Labelliere's motives for his curious burial, nor how he was able to predict months in advance the precise day on which he would die.

The grave of Major Peter Labelliere is not easy to find as there are no signposts to it. It lies just east of the Old Fort, on the top of Box Hill along a path through woodland.

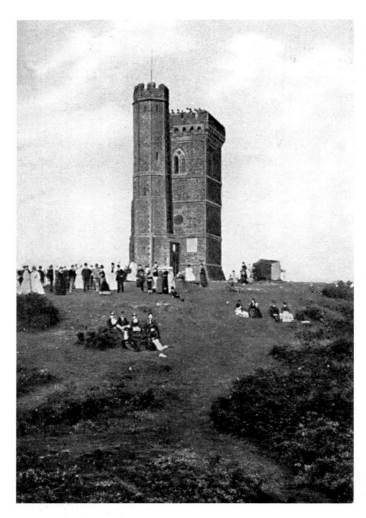

Leith Hill is topped by a tower which was built to raise the summit of the hill to the status of a mountain, but which was later used for a very different and altogether more macabre purpose.

Another odd burial was that of Richard Hull at Leith Hill, also near Dorking. In the eighteenth century, Hull was the owner of Leith Hill Place, the estate of which included the hill. Leith Hill is 965ft tall and the geographers of the day had a rule that a hill was any elevation up to 1,000ft tall, and a mountain was a peak over 1,000ft tall. Hull accordingly built a tower 64ft tall so that the peak would be over 1,000ft and Leith Hill would qualify to be a mountain. Sadly the geographers did not fall for this ruse and the name of Leith Mountain never caught on.

Nevertheless, Hull was very proud of his tower and opened it up to the public so that they could enjoy the views. He himself spent many hours there and when he died in 1772, left a will stating that he wished to be buried beneath the tower. The desire to be buried outside consecrated ground was considered bizarre enough in the eighteenth century, but his stipulation that he be buried on his horse was quite outrageous. In the event, the horse was not interred on the hilltop, but Hull was and he remains there still.

Rather more enigmatic than the bizarre burials are the Chobham Treacle Mines. These fabulous mines have been rumoured to exist up on Chobham Common since at least the First World War. The most often cited location is near Round Pond, north of Burrowhill. The most usual version of the story has it that the treacle is not found in a mine in the conventional sense of the word, but forms a natural spring where it bubbles up out of the ground. The 'mines' are shafts sunk by greedy locals trying in vain to get to the source of the treacle.

Quite how the treacle got to Chobham Common is a matter of dispute. One theory had it that in ages past, the climate in Britain was very much hotter than it is today – a fact that cannot be denied – and that in those distant days, sugar cane grew luxuriantly across Surrey. The cane grew, fell and rotted on the ground, allowing the sugar-rich juice to drain away down through the sands of the common until it struck an impermeable clay layer deep below the ground. There it gathered and matured into treacle.

Another version had it that the treacle had its origins in 1853. In that year, a force of 8,000 soldiers gathered on Chobham Common to parade and go through manoeuvres prior to setting off for the Crimean War. They stayed there for eight weeks and the highlight of the event came with a Royal review in front of Queen Victoria. When the soldiers marched off to war, they left behind them a stock of unused supplies, among which were thirty hogsheads of treacle. The lazy waggoners could not be bothered to move the barrels, so tipped them into a convenient hollow and covered them over with rubble and soil. The barrels subsequently split and the treacle oozed out to form an apparent spring of treacle.

Chobham Common is an extensive area of sandy heath which, unlike much Surrey heathland, has escaped being built over for housing. It is somewhere here that the famous Treacle Mines are said to exist.

Other locals dismiss this story as nonsense and instead insist that the treacle was left behind by a force of American soldiers who camped on the common in 1917 on their way to the trenches of the First World War in France.

Whatever the origins of the spring of treacle and the subsequent mines, the flow seems to have been stopped when the M3 was built over the common. Presumably the construction works somehow disrupted the fissures in the subsoil through which the treacle flowed. That said, there are those who believe that the treacle is slowly oozing its way through the sands and may erupt in a fresh spring any day now. Who knows who will be the lucky person out walking over Chobham Common on the day that the treacle re-emerges.

A liquid of a very different kind formerly oozed from a tomb at Wonersh. The church, dedicated to St John the Baptist, is a pretty medieval church, parts of which date back to the eleventh century. The church stands beside the river, but the bizarre liquid has nothing to do with the stream. The so-called 'Weeping Tomb' is a table-top structure decorated with brass shields that stands beside the screen to the chancel. It is made of marble and dates to the sixteenth century.

Nobody knows when it began to weep, but the mysterious manifestation was certainly occurring by the later eighteenth century. Each year in early October, a sticky brown liquid would begin to seep out of a crack near the base of the tomb. The viscous fluid would flow for a couple of weeks, then cease – until the following October.

Traffic thunders along the stretch of the M3 that crosses Chobham Common. It was the building of this road that allegedly caused the Treacle Mines to dry up, at least temporarily.

The charmingly
rural Wonersh
Church hides
a mystery in
the form of the
famous 'Weeping
Tomb'.

Theories have long abounded as to what this was. Some suggested that it was cassia, a type of embalming fluid containing cinnamon that was used in former centuries. Why it should flow and dry up so regularly was never explained, though perhaps it had something to do with the chill weather and wet atmosphere of autumn. Others suggested that it was caused by some hidden water source under the church that intermittently raised the water table, initiating the flow when the autumn rains came. Others said it was the tomb weeping on the anniversary of the death of its occupant.

In truth, nobody knows what the liquid was nor why the tomb wept so regularly. It is unlikely that we shall ever find out. In the 1950s, the church was the subject of various repairs and modernisations, in the course of which the crack in the marble of the Weeping Tomb was cemented over. The tomb weeps no more.

Another tomb with an odd story attached is in St Mary's at Stoke D'Abernon. Some 250 years ago, the D'Abernon estates were in the possession of the wealthy Vincent family. The lord of the manor was out shooting on Fairmile Common with his younger brother one day. In those days, birds were not beaten toward the guns, as today, but the hunters stalked the birds using dogs to flush them out into the air so that they could be shot. The two men found plenty of birds, but neither of them had been able to shoot a single one. In a ferocious temper, the younger Vincent swore savagely that he would unfailingly shoot the next thing that his dogs put up from a patch of undergrowth. The dogs merrily plunged into a thicket, driving out not a pheasant, but the miller from the adjacent hamlet of Downside. The younger Vincent brother lifted his gun and shot the miller.

The horrified elder brother ran to the prostrate miller, and instructed the younger brother to help him. The miller was stone dead, but in trying to lift the poor man the younger brother got his hand deeply stained with blood – a mark that would never come off, no matter how hard he scrubbed. The younger brother was bundled off to hide in a folly on the estate while the elder went to work to hush up the matter. The miller's family were offered a large sum of money to accept an invented story about a hunting accident, while the local magistrate was put off and delayed until the locals could be got on side. The conspiracy was doomed to failure and word soon leaked out about what had really happened. The younger brother died rather conveniently at this point and was buried at St Mary's with a bloody hand painted on his tomb as a mark of his guilt.

St Mary's Church at Stoke D'Abernon is the burial place of a local landowner who, if local legend is to be believed, was guilty of a brutal and most callous murder.

The rock that stands beside the gates to Pyford Court has a curious legend attached to it. The stone served for centuries as a boundary marker for the parish, but is thought by some to be a relic of ancient pagan religion and to have stood here for at least 4,000 years.

Rather less ominous is the rock by the gates to Pyrford Court. The story behind this enigmatic stone is lost in time; all that anyone can recall about it now is that it can move by itself. On mornings when a cock crows on the precise moment when the sun first peeps over the eastern horizon, the rock lifts itself up out of the ground, turns around and sinks back into place.

Of all the bizarre paranormal events to strike Surrey, none could be stranger than the long-running saga of Spring Heeled Jack. This character has, in the twentieth century, featured in at least one horror movie and several fictional books, but to the nineteenth-century inhabitants of Surrey he was a very solid and utterly terrifying reality.

There are incomplete and infrequent accounts of an entity who might be Spring Heeled Jack from as early as 1817, but it was twenty years later that his activities really began. On 9 January 1838 the Lord Mayor of London, Sir John Cowan, revealed to a meeting of city aldermen a letter that he had received a few days earlier. He said that he had at first kept the contents secret while investigations were carried out, but since these had proved fruitless he was enlisting the help of the aldermen. The letter had come from Peckham – then a pleasant semi-rural Surrey village on the outskirts of London that was in the process of being swallowed up by suburbs. The letter was unsigned and the postmistress of Peckham did not recall who had handed the letter in. It was presumed that it must have been a local for the woman might have remembered a stranger.

The letter alleged that a gentleman of high rank and wealth had made a bet with 'a mischievous and foolhardy companion' the previous autumn. The wager aimed to scare thirty people to death. In the process the man was:

> … to visit many of the villages near London in three different disguises – a ghost, a bear, and a devil, and moreover, enter a gentleman gardens for the purpose of alarming the inmates of the house. The wager has been accepted, and the unmanly villain has succeeded in depriving seven ladies of their senses. The affair has now been going on for some time and, strange to say, the papers are still silent on the subject. The writer of this letter has reason to believe that they have the whole history at their fingerends, but through interested motives are induced to remain silent.

The story was soon carried in the London newspapers, along with an appeal for news of the villainous gentleman. Reports flooded in to both the Lord Mayor and to the newspapers. At first the stories related to events over the previous weeks, which served to excite public interest, but were of little help to the police as the culprit was long gone and witnesses memories were often vague or conflicting. In one place the mysterious intruder had taken the form of a gigantic baboon, in another he had clanked about in medieval armour, in a third he looked more like a white bull than anything else and a fourth witness described him as a white bear. The various sightings came from southern London and from a number of towns and villages of northern Surrey and northern Kent. The strange figure seemed to like it south of the Thames.

One account stood out from the rest as it had been reported to police at the time it took place. In October 1837, a seventeen-year-old serving girl named Polly Adams had been given the day off work to go to Blackheath Fair with some friends. At one point she fell into conversation with a tall, aristocratic man. Something about the gentleman put her off, and anyway she was there to have fun with her friends, so she turned her back and walked off. At dusk, as Polly and her friends left the fair, they were set upon by a tall man who gave the unfortunate Polly a hefty blow before fleeing into the gathering night.

The police soon established that Henry Beresford, the Marquis of Waterford, had been at the fair that day. He was a tall, aristocratic-looking man and had a reputation both for seducing young women and for being violent when drunk. However, neither Polly nor any of her friends could positively identify Waterford and the matter was dropped.

On only one thing were many of these early accounts agreed – the bizarre apparition could leap huge distances. He had been seen jumping over walls 10ft tall, crossing a street from pavement to pavement in a single stride or bounding along with gigantic leaps faster than any normal man could run. It was theorised that the gentleman of wealth who was behind the appearances was able to achieve these feats by having placed enormously strong springs in the heels of his boots – and so the strange figure acquired his name of Spring Heeled Jack.

On the evening of 18 February, two sisters, eighteen-year-old Lucy Scales and her younger sister, Margaret, were walking home from visiting their brother, a butcher in Limehouse. Lucy was a couple of steps ahead of her sister when she walked past the entrance to an alley. A figure sprang out at her and grabbed her by the shoulders. A sheet of flame leapt from the figure's mouth, and Lucy fell down in a fit. Her sister ran to her help as the attacker bounded off down the street with gigantic strides. Lucy recovered in a few minutes and a passer-by who had seen the attack summoned a policeman. The assailant had, however, gone.

Two days later three teenage girls – Jane, Sarah and Mary Alsop – were at home alone one evening when there came a thunderous knocking at the front door of their family home in East London. The eldest, eighteen-year-old Jane, opened the door to see a tall man in a dark cloak. He seemed agitated. 'For God's sake bring me a light,' he demanded. 'We have caught Spring Heeled Jack in the lane'.

Jane went to get a lit candle and returned to the door with it. At this point, the man threw back his cloak to reveal a bizarre costume. He was clad in a skin-tight suit of white oilskin, topped with a large helmet. His eyes began to glow red like coal embers. From his mouth came a sheet of blue flames which poured forth over the girl's face. Closing her eyes in alarm, Jane felt her arms grabbed by vice-like hands, then talons clawed at her dress, tearing it from her body and inflicting nasty scratches on her arms and shoulders.

The commotion brought Sarah and Mary running to their sister's defence. Sarah managed to slam the door while Mary pulled Jane back into the house. Peering from the windows to assure themselves the attacker had gone, the girls ran for a neighbour who summoned both the police and a doctor. Jane's injuries proved not to be serious, while the police had no luck catching the terrifying culprit.

A week later, another young girl answered the door to a man in a cloak. She was taking no chances and slammed the door shut in the stranger's face. She later told police that she thought she had seen the letter 'W' picked out in gold thread on a jacket under the cloak. The clue did not help much.

For several weeks the fire-breathing figure of a man in a cloak or in tightly-fitted white oilskins was seen in several places at night. Everywhere it was seen, the figure spread alarm and fear, inflicting minor, but painful, injuries whenever it could and breathing white or blue flames with abandon. In the late spring of 1838 the attacks seem to have ceased. Reports and sightings continued to be made, but these were less detailed and at a greater distance than before. Whoever or whatever Spring Heeled Jack had been, he seemed to have stopped his attacks.

Then, in 1845, he was back with a vengeance. A figure with horns on his head was seen bounding to incredible heights over hedges and walls in west London. A local butcher with a reputation for practical jokes was arrested and bound over to keep the peace, but there was little evidence that he was guilty – and in any case, the appearances continued. The high-leaping, fire breather Jack was spotted across London. In the autumn he claimed his first victim when he attacked a thirteen-year-old girl named Maria Davis on a bridge over an open sewer in the East End. The girl fell off the bridge while trying to escape, struck her head and drowned before anyone could pull her out of the muddy, filthy water. Sightings continued now and then, but in 1872 a fresh outbreak of intense activity began.

This new phase lasted five years and culminated in a series of attacks at Aldershot. A sentry on evening duty on the perimeter of North Camp sighted a figure bounding across the common toward him. The stranger seemed to be leaping with ease over gorse bushes and other obstructions. A soft glow emitted from the figure. The sentry shouted a challenge when the figure was about 20yds away, whereupon the mystery man vanished. Several tense seconds ticked by as the sentry peered into the night. Suddenly the strange figure was standing right next to the startled soldier. The intruder slapped the sentry around the face with a hand as cold and clammy as that of a corpse, then bounded off across the common to disappear from sight in a series of gigantic leaps.

The strange nocturnal attacker was seen off and on in the weeks that followed. One sentry fired at him at point blank range, but with no effect and a rumour spread that Spring Heeled Jack was invulnerable to firearms. After leaving Aldershot, Spring Heeled Jack was seen in Cheshire and Liverpool. Then he went away and never came back.

Even while Spring Heeled Jack was making real appearances, he was featuring in fiction. Numerous cheap novels and short stories – the famous 'penny dreadfuls' – were published in which Spring Heeled Jack was the principal villain. In these stories he was sometimes a real man with springs in his heels, but more often he was some supernatural horror monster or demon come to earth to wreak violence and terror on humanity. By the late nineteenth century, Spring Heeled Jack was sometimes being portrayed as the hero, righting wrongs and punishing villains that the police could not catch. In 1946 he was portrayed as a crazed lord intent on mayhem in the horror movie *Curse of the Wraydons*. Jack was played by the great melodramatic stage actor, Tod Slaughter, who specialised in such roles.

Over the years, many suggestions have been put forward to explain Spring Heeled Jack. With hindsight it would seem that there were a number of outbreaks of activity. The first, in 1838-39, featured a tall man in costly clothing who could jump huge distances and who could spurt blue fire from his mouth. He was seen across the southern suburbs of London and in nearby villages in Surrey and Kent. In 1845 a similar figure was seen in London, though he seemed to lack the leaping abilities of his predecessor. The 1870s saw the return of the ability to leap huge distances, but the fire-breathing had gone. In between these periods of intense activity there had been less frequent sightings, many of which were vague or untrustworthy.

Some have suggested that Spring Heeled Jack was a real human, or rather two or three humans. The Jack of 1838 is often said to have been the Marquis of Waterford. He was certainly inclined to such jokes and to violence. He was athletic and could have pranced about in a fashion that an overexcited person might have taken for progressing in supernaturally large jumps. He almost certainly attacked Polly Adams and he did have a 'W' embroidered on some of his clothes, as one witness reported. The Jack of 1845 may have been Waterford, but he was not in London at the time of all the reported sightings. He certainly was not the Jack of the 1870s as he had died in 1859. Perhaps the later Jacks were imitators.

Other theories discount the idea that a human could have been responsible. It has been suggested that Spring Heeled Jack may have been a demon or evil spirit. He certainly inflicted violence on those he attacked and one person died as a result of his activities. More recent studies have highlighted the similarities between Spring Heeled Jack's activities in the open air and those of some entities emerging from UFOs. The truth behind this bizarre series of events will probably never be known.

An unexpected sequel to the story of Spring Heeled Jack came on 28 July 1963 in Caterham, near the junction of the A22 with Croydon Road. At 10 p.m., a number of motorists saw several men – some said as few as three, others as many as eight – dressed in black cloaks and hoods. The men were running and leaping about with apparently supernatural heights and speeds. The police were called, but by the time they arrived the strange leaping figures had gone. Was Spring Heeled Jack back? If he was, he did not hang about. This was the only sighting.

SEVEN

FAIRIES, GIANTS AND OTHERS

It is fashionable to scoff at tales about fairies and giants, or to consign them to books intended for young children. This is not an error our forefathers would have made. They knew that the little people were very real denizens of Surrey – and that they had to be treated with proper respect.

The real fairies of past centuries were not gossamer-winged sprites engaged in painting flowers pretty colours or prancing about among the dew. They were a powerful tribe of diminutive humans, around 3ft tall, who had the gift of flight and lived in the wilder areas of rural Surrey. They had the ability to mislead humans, making them see and hear what the fairies wanted. They could steal away babies, ruin crops and turn butter sour. They could help humans or harm them according to their whims and capricious nature. Fairies had the gift of glamour, meaning that they appeared to be handsome, rich and charming even when intent on the most hideous of evil acts.

All in all, they were best avoided, but if that were not possible it was wise to placate them. In Surrey it was considered bad luck to call the fairies by their true name, so they were usually referred to as Farisees, which could be confused with the Pharisees of the Bible by outsiders.

One of the pranks that the Farisees like to indulge in was to remove livestock from barns or fields at night and ride them at high speed until they were exhausted and covered in sweat. Then the hapless creature would be returned to the barn or field for the farmer to find it next morning. Whenever a horse, cow or pig was found in a sweat in the morning, the farmer knew that it had been 'Farisee ridden'. The only cure for this was to hang a flint on a piece of string so that it dangled just over the back of the animal in question. Farisees did not care for flint, so the stone would stop them getting onto the animal.

More practical folk might consider that an animal found to be all sweaty and exhausted in the morning might have been suffering from a fever, but traditional beliefs were slow to die. As late as 1920, a vet based in Guildford was called out to minister to a sick calf and found a flint dangling over its stall. 'Best to be safe, you see', explained the unabashed farmer.

At other times the Farisees could be more favourably disposed towards the humans of Surrey. Talking to the curate at Puttenham in 1869, an old man recalled an incident from his youth. He had been hired by a local farmer and given the task of threshing the wheat stored in the barn – a tough job of arduous physical labour. He set to work on the task that he expected to keep him busy for a couple of weeks, but on his second morning he found that a quantity of the grain had been threshed during the night. The man asked the other hands, but nobody had done the work.

The next day, he again found that some of his work had been done during the night, but again nobody claimed the credit. Determined to find out who was helping him, the man pretended to leave at dusk, but in fact sneaked back into the barn and clambered up into the roof beams. There he could get a clear view of the barn without himself being seen.

In the nineteenth century, the curate at Puttenham Church was told a story about the local fairies by an elderly farm worker.

Soon after midnight, the door of the barn creaked open and the glimmer of a lantern was seen. As the man watched he saw two diminutive men, no more than 3ft tall, enter the barn. Each man carried with him a small threshing flail of a size suitable for his build. Without a word, the two men set to work. The grain was being threshed at a considerable rate. After an hour or so one of the little men stopped work, turned to his companion and said, 'I sweat. Do you?'

Up on his perch in the rafters, the farmworker muttered, 'Yes and the Devil sweat both of you'. The little men obviously heard him, for they both looked up angrily at the roof. Picking up their flails the men left, and never again did the Farisees do a good turn for the man, nor for the farmer who had employed him.

The Puttenham farmhand got off lightly compared to Matthew Trigg. In the early eighteenth century, Trigg was a cantankerous old codger who lived at Ash. One day the villagers noticed he was missing. Some children had seen him set off for a walk in the woods between Ash and Tongham. A search party set off, but there was no sign of him other than his walking stick, found discarded among the trees. Worried, the villagers consulted the local wise woman, or witch. She poured pure spring water into a brightly-polished copper basin and sat staring at it for a while.

'The Farisees have him,' she finally declared. 'He came across them dancing in the woods and the old fool spoke to them. Now they have him far away to the east and have put an enchantment on him to make him dance forever for their amusement. If we don't rescue him soon he will die of exhaustion.'

In answer to the demands of the villagers that something be done, the wise woman asked each of them to donate a small personal item that they were willing to give to get Matthew Trigg back again. One woman gave a hair ribbon, a child donated a doll and a man gave a whistle. The wise woman put all the items into a pot and set them on fire. She then collected the ashes and mixed them with some goose fat. Taking the resulting mixture outside, she smeared it on the head of her old horse, then whispered the name 'Matthew Trigg' in the horse's ear. The horse gave a whinny, and set off at a trot.

'Now we wait,' said the old woman. Everyone sat down as the time passed. A few hours later, there came a whinny. The people looked about, but could see no horse. Then they realised that the wise woman was looking upward. Coming toward them through the air was the old horse with a terrified Matthew Trigg hanging on for dear life. The horse seemed to be having trouble flying in a straight line and at one point it collided with the steeple of Ash Church, its hooves inflicting a dramatic dent on the side of the spire. Then it came down to earth and Matthew Trigg was saved.

The hoof marks remained on Ash Church steeple until 1864, when an unimaginative new vicar had the old spire replaced with a flawless new one, which remains to this day.

Perhaps the best known tale relating to the Farisees of Surrey concerns the old cauldron kept in Frensham Church. The story was first set down in 1686 by the antiquarian John Aubrey, rather better known for his work on Stonehenge. According to Aubrey, the cauldron was kept in the church after it was acquired due to a broken promise between the human folk of Frensham and their Farisee neighbours. Perhaps it was considered that the sacred confine of the church was the only safe place for such a powerful magical fairy item.

According to Aubrey, there had for centuries been an ongoing arrangement between the humans and fairies of Frensham. The fairies lived in 'Borough Hill', which Aubrey said was a mile or so from Frensham Church in the direction of 'Cherte' (now Churt). The hill was marked by a large boulder close to a cave. The cave marked the entrance to the domain of the

The steeple on the church at Ash was replaced after an encounter with the little people left it with a large dent and pronounced list.

fairies and when Aubrey visited there were plenty of people willing to tell him that they had heard the music of the fairies' dancing coming from the cave, but had been wise enough not to enter. It did not do to disturb the little folk at their revels.

In years past, the fairies had been willing to lend some of their possessions to the humans. To borrow something from the little folk, the humans had to walk to the great boulder on Borough Hill and knock on it with their fist. The person then had to shout out what it was they wanted to borrow – be it a plough, yoke of oxen, some cash, an anvil or another useful item. If the fairies were willing to lend the item, a voice would boom out of the cave laying down the conditions of the trade. The voice would stipulate for how long the item could be borrowed, when it had to be returned and if the fairies wanted anything in return. This was usually some inexpensive item such as the first sheaf of wheat harvested on the land of the borrower, or perhaps a basket of flowers.

If the would-be borrower agreed, he had to shout out this fact. Then he had to turn and walk away without a backward glance – presumably to avoid seeing the little people. The human had to return at dawn the following day when he would find the desired item set down beside the stone.

This useful arrangement went on for generations. Then, one fateful day, a Frensham farmer borrowed a great cauldron in which to cook a great stew to be served at his daughter's wedding. The cauldron was to be returned at sunset. Unfortunately, what with all the rejoicing, celebrations and drinking going on, the farmer did not return the cauldron by the agreed time. Realising that he would be late, the man and a friend ran as fast as they could from Frensham to Borough Hill carrying the cauldron between them. They got to the stone just seconds after the sun had gone down. Hoping they were in time, they left the cauldron on the stone as tradition demanded. Next morning, it was still there. The Farisees had not retrieved it. Thereafter, no borrowing took place for the little people refused to have any further dealings with the people of Frensham. And so the cauldron came to rest in the church.

There are a few problems with the story as set down by Aubrey. There is, for a start, no such place as Borough Hill a mile from Frensham Church. There is a Redborough Hill, but that is more than three miles to the east and it has neither a cave nor an obvious boulder. There is a hill almost two miles south-east from the church that does have a prominent boulder lying on its flank. Two miles south-east is not so very different from Aubrey's mile south, but it is not an exact fit. Up on Frensham Common, a mile from the church, are to be found a number of ancient burial mounds, known as barrows, which are made out of boulders, turf and soil and that date back around 5,000 years. In other parts of England, similar mounds are often linked to the little people, so it may be that Aubrey meant one of these, though none of them have a cave.

Frensham Church features in a long and involved legend that embraces fairies, witches and even the Devil himself. Nobody knows how much of the story is true, but the church houses an ancient cauldron that is at the centre of the tale.

By the year 1800, the story of the Frensham Cauldron had changed somewhat. The fairies were no longer mentioned and instead the paranormal lender of the borrowed items was an immensely powerful witch called Mother Ludlam. Her home was not the missing Borough Hill, but the ornamental grotto in the grounds of Moor Park to the north-east of Frensham. Despite this change of personnel and venue, the story was much the same.

By 1900, the Devil had entered the tale. In this version it was the Evil One, not some local farmer, who borrowed Mother Ludlam's cauldron. His intention was to steal it, but his nefarious purpose was discovered by the witch who gave chase and caught up with Satan in the skies over Frensham. In the fight that followed, the cauldron slipped from the Devil's fingers and landed in the churchyard. Neither demon nor witch could enter the holy ground to retrieve it, so the villagers kept the item and lodged it in the church. Thus may a story change and evolve over time.

If the identity of the Frensham Cauldron's original owner is unclear, so is the true nature of the beautiful damsel of the Silent Pool. This beauty spot lies just off the A25, a mile west of Shere, and today has its own car park. This striking pool of crystal clear water nestles beneath towering trees at the foot of the downs. It is a famously charming spot which tempts motorists passing on the A25 as much as it does the more energetic walkers on the North Downs Way, which runs along the crest of the hills half a mile to the north. The pure waters come from rain which falls on the North Downs and spends years soaking down through the chalk before striking a layer of impervious clay and being forced to the surface.

Elsewhere the springs form small streams, but here the waters are caught by a ridge of sandstone and form a delightful, tear-shaped pond. Sheltered by the trees and the hills, the spot is charmingly quiet. On occasion, the birds and the breeze fall still and the Silent Pool truly lives up to its name.

This peaceful scene is sometimes disturbed, local legend has it, by a most beautiful and mysterious figure. Entirely naked, the spirit washes herself and swims playfully before diving into the waters and disappearing from sight.

Who she might be is not clear. According to a version of the story first written down a century and a half ago, the beautiful young woman was a local peasant girl named Emma who lived here in the early thirteenth century. She was in the habit of bathing in the clear waters of the Silent Pool, but one day a nobleman rode by and saw her. Overcome with lust for the pretty farm girl, the nobleman splashed into the Silent Pool in an attempt to grab the girl and drag her ashore. Rather than give in to his decidedly improper advances, the girl waded into deeper water, slipped and drowned. The girl's cries attracted her father, who arrived too late to save his daughter, but in time to see the evil nobleman ride off.

Although this version of the girl's tragic fate seems to be widely believed in the area, it is sadly untrue. The evil nobleman and his unwelcome advances were invented by the writer Martin Tupper in a short story he wrote in 1858. In this story, set in the early thirteenth century, the nobleman is identified as King John from a cap he dropped at the scene of his crime. The local priest takes the cap to Stephen Langton, Archbishop of Canterbury, who was born nearby at Friday Street. Langton uses the evidence of the cap to sway the barons against King John. The King's crime becomes the basis for the doctrine that nobody, not even the King, is above the law. This doctrine is then enshrined in Magna Carta by the outraged Langton and the barons.

The Silent Pool has a most alluring phantom, though she may be more powerful than she at first appears and is best treated with respect.

A good story, but sadly it is nonsense. Langton was born in Lincolnshire, not Surrey, and he had nothing whatsoever to do with the vicar at Shere. Moreover, whatever motives the barons had for drawing up Magna Carta, the plight of a peasant girl was not among them. Nor is there any historical record of King John ever molesting a peasant girl – though in truth, he did many shocking things. Tupper simply invented the tale and grafted it on to the local legend of the attractive phantom.

This leaves us to wonder who the beautiful maiden of the Silent Pool actually is. She may indeed be a poor drowned local girl, but there is a more interesting theory. Water sources, such as the Silent Pool, were sacred to the beautiful water goddesses of the pagan past. It is clear that the more atmospheric the place – and the Silent Pool is nothing if not atmospheric – the more sacred the spring was considered. Could it be that the beautiful ghost of the Silent Pool is simply the half-forgotten memory of a powerful pagan goddess?

We know that before Christianity came to England, the pagan English believed in not only the great gods, but also in a multitude of local spirits and paranormal entities. Natural landscape features each had their own minor deity or spirit to stand guard over them and care for their well-being. Water features tended to attract beautiful young goddesses, so it is reasonable to assume that a water feature as noticeable as the Silent Pool would have been the home of such a lovely deity. Perhaps she lives there still.

In most versions of the legend of the Silent Pool, King John features as the villain of the piece. Sadly, there is no evidence that he ever visited the place.

According to an ancient legend, the chapel on top of St Catherine's Hill, just south of Guildford, was constructed by a monstrous, but kindly, giantess engaged in a building competition with her sister who lived on nearby St Martha's Hill.

Rather different from the Farisees, the little people, were the giants. There are not too many of these folk in Surrey, but two giantesses did live in Guildford. One had her home on St Martha's Hill and the other St Catherine's Hill. Each decided that they wanted to demonstrate their Christian piety by building a holy establishment. The giantess on St Martha's Hill opted for a church, her sister on St Catherine's Hill decided on a priory. Being giantesses, the sisters had no trouble heaving the stones, timbers and other materials up to the hill summits, but they did lack tools. In fact, they had only one hammer between them. The two giantesses took to throwing the hammer back and forth from hilltop to hilltop as each needed the tool.

As for the unfortunate humans who had to live with a gigantic hammer flying through the sky over their heads day after day, they got to be very good at ducking.

EIGHT

POLTERGEISTS

The word 'poltergeist' is German for 'noisy ghost', but that does not even begin to describe the range of activities that these entities get up to, nor the sheer terror that they can inspire. When the director of a horror movie is looking for ghostly events with which to scare his audience, it is to the poltergeist that he turns. Their ability to terrify and persecute is endless and their tricky malevolence beyond dispute.

Poltergeists have gone by various names in the past. They have been thought to be a wicked tribe of fairies, being called boggles or boggarts. Others have thought they are demons from Hell, or familiar spirits sent by witches and wizards to wreak havoc. These days, the disturbances are subjected to more scientific enquiry and more rational explanations sought – though not often with any real success.

Poltergeists come in many forms and their activities can be astonishingly diverse. What links all the cases is that unseen hands move objects, create noises and generally make a nuisance of themselves in a particular house or place of work. Some poltergeists content themselves with childish pranks, others indulge in the full panoply of terror.

In 1977 a story broke in the county press about a poltergeist in Merrow that had reduced the targeted family to a state of abject terror. The Fairweathers lived in a quite unremarkable council house in Finches Rise – a three-bedroom house of the 1950s. The family consisted of Mr and Mrs Fairweather, their daughter and her husband, and their two children; a young boy and an older girl.

The poltergeist visitation began slowly, so much so that it was only with hindsight that the Fairweathers realised that anything had been going on at all. Mr Fairweather put his watch down in one place when he went to bed, but found it somewhere else when he woke up. Mrs Fairweather had persistent trouble finding her keys as they were never where she had left them. Kitchen utensils went missing and simply could not be found, then a couple of days later they would turn up in full view on the kitchen work surface. Then the chills began. A room would suddenly become bitterly cold, remain like that for a few seconds and then return to normal.

The Fairweathers slowly realised that the chills came when an object was moved or went missing. In the bathroom one evening, Mr Fairweather felt the chill descend and sensed something behind him. Grabbing a towel, he spun around and lashed out. Whatever was causing the chill left abruptly and the temperature returned to normal. Mr Fairweather got into the habit of stomping around the house in the evening – the time of day when most incidents occurred – waving his towel about and ordering the thing to leave his family alone. It often worked, but sometimes did not.

Getting to their wits end, but not certain how to go about solving their problems, the Fairweathers turned to the Church. A priest visited and held a blessing service, but it did no good. The poltergeist was quiet during the proceedings but was back the next day. Gradually the disturbances got more and more serious. Larger objects began to be moved about, chairs and tables, and the chill came more and more often.

It all came to a head in late May 1977 on an evening when a thunderstorm was rumbling around in the distance. The two children were put to bed and the four adults were downstairs having supper when the chill came. Then the boy screamed in terror. The adults raced upstairs to find him sitting upright in bed, almost gibbering with fright. 'Take him away, take him away,' he repeated over and over again, staring at a corner of the room. There was nobody and nothing there. The adults picked up the boy and his sister and hastened back downstairs. While the men took it in turns to keep watch, the others slept fitfully.

When the boy had calmed down sufficiently, he was asked what he had seen that had frightened him so much. He reported that he had woken up to find a strange man in the room. The man was tall, dressed in a shapeless black cloak and a black hat. The boy said that the man had a frightening face, but could not give any precise details.

One of the apparently perfectly normal houses in Finches Rise, Merrow, played host to a most disturbing poltergeist that hit the news headlines in 1977.

Chilworth's Percy Arms was the home of a particularly long-lived poltergeist that apparently maintained its energy for over 10 years — far longer than the usual span of a poltergeist visitation.

Next day the family moved out to stay temporarily with friends while the council found them a new home. There was, at first, some suspicion that the Fairweathers may have been making up the story in order to move out of their overcrowded three bedroom house. But these ideas were quickly dispelled by Mrs Fairweather. 'We will move anywhere and accept anything,' she declared. And they did, moving into a house barely any bigger than the one they had vacated so hurriedly.

The newspapers got hold of the story and sought an answer. A local historian came up with one idea. The area north of Merrow village, where the estate had been built, had formerly been an empty stretch of heathland known as Ganghill Common. On 26 August 1776, three local criminals were executed there by being hanged from a gallows. James Potter was a highwayman who preyed on coaches and riders crossing the downs. Frederick Gregg was what would today be termed a mugger, attacking people at night with a club and knife to steal anything they had on them. Christopher Ellis was a burglar who broke into houses and beat up the occupants to force them to reveal the location of their valuables.

The historian speculated that the gallows may have stood on the site of the house in Finches Rise and that the poltergeist was the returning spirit of one of the men hanged there. If this were the case, there seemed no reason why the ghost had not manifested itself in the decades since the execution, nor why it should cease to walk as soon as the Fairweathers left the house.

Another poltergeist most active in the 1970s was the entity nicknamed 'George' who took up residence in the Percy Arms at Chilworth. This poltergeist failed to inspire terror, more curiosity and puzzlement. The visitation seems to have begun in the late 1960s, though again it began with minor incidents that were only recognised as being paranormal with hindsight. The landlady since the 1950s was a Mrs Testar. For some years the poltergeist contented itself with moving objects about during the night. Mrs Testar would come down in the morning to find chairs and tables all pushed to one end of the bar, or that the glasses had all been carefully removed from their places and set up on the tables. It was all a bit of a nuisance, but no more than that.

In the 1970s, things began to become more serious. Doors would open by themselves and then be slammed shut with terrific force. The shutters over the bar would be rattled violently and noisily by unseen hands, waking up everyone sleeping at the pub. Then things began to move when people were present. Perhaps the first object to do this was a chair which was seen to shoot backwards across the bar room floor as if somebody had been sitting in it and had then stood up suddenly, but there was nobody near the chair at the time who could have caused it to move. Other chairs and tables were seen to move about, but they would usually stop moving as soon as anyone turned to look at them. It was as if whatever was doing the moving wanted to attract attention and, having done so, was content.

Then glasses began to shift about. Beer tankards were the most often moved. They would levitate from wherever they were, drift silently across the room, and then settle down on a table or, sometimes, on the floor. One thing that was noticed was that although the glasses often moved very quickly as if they had been thrown, they never broke. It was as if the glasses were being carried and placed down with care. The sole exception came when Mrs Testar served her cousin with a pint of beer. She was telling him about the latest phantom incidents when the foaming glass of beer suddenly slid off along the bar with ever-increasing speed. It flew off the far end and smashed against the wall, spraying beer everywhere.

Once again the local press got involved and began to seek a ghostly origin for the poltergeist. There were no tragedies nor sudden deaths linked to the pub, but there had been an inquest held there in 1901 into a terrible local tragedy. The pub seems to have been used as it had the largest room available for hire in the village.

On 12 February 1901, an explosion had taken place at the Chilworth Gunpowder Mill, which used the nearby River Tillingbourne for power. The blast had killed six men and had so badly damaged the workroom where they had been that it was impossible to identify any cause for the blast. All safety procedures had been in place and were being followed carefully. Perhaps it had just been bad luck. One of the men had survived the initial blast, but died within hours. His name had been George Smithers. Once the press had retold the story of the blast, Mrs Testar and the pub regulars took to calling the poltergeist 'George'.

The disturbances continued for a few months, then began to fade in intensity and by the late 1970s had ceased altogether.

Ham House near Richmond would appear to have a poltergeist with a rather singular fixation. In the Tollemarche Room is kept a wheelchair for the use of visitors to the property. It has often been reported moving about of its own accord, sometimes even rolling out into the corridor as if seeking a person to whom it could be useful.

Another pub to be plagued by a poltergeist for a while was the Queens Head Pub, Weybridge, during the later 1990s. When a new landlord, Phil Emery, moved in on 8 May 1997, the place already had a reputation for being haunted. The activity was generally of a low-level poltergeist nature. Bottles, glasses and other small objects were put down in one place, but found to be somewhere quite different a few minutes later. Irritating and spooky, certainly, but not especially frightening.

Soon after Emery moved in, things began to increase in tempo. He was first aware of something odd one night a few weeks after he moved in. He had locked up for the night and gone upstairs when he heard the unmistakable sounds of someone walking about downstairs. Footsteps moved across the floor, doors opened and shut. Not sure whether he was dealing with a burglar or a customer he had inadvertently locked in, Emery ventured down the stairs. The sounds of movement came from the bar, but as he entered, Emery heard the noises retreat to the gents' toilets. Warily pushing the door open, he found the room to be completely empty. However, the hand dryer was blowing at full blast as if somebody had just pushed the button to set it going.

The activity gradually got more frequent and more dramatic over the months that followed. Towards the end of the year, two figures began to be seen. The first was a woman who was glimpsed only vaguely or fleetingly. She seemed to be dressed in a long gown, probably of an old-fashioned cut. She was seen infrequently, but was associated with the more violent actions of the poltergeist. When glasses were smashed or tables danced around the room, the female figure was present most often. The second figure was that of an elderly man. He seemed rather calmer than the woman and was seen at least once in considerable detail. He was once visible sitting on a bench in the bar. He was wearing a black jacket, grey trousers and a white scarf, and had heavy workman-style boots on his feet.

Once Christmas 1999 was over, the manifestations went into a gradual, but steady, decline. By the year 2002, the haunting seemed to have ceased.

The stories of some other poltergeists active in Surrey over the years came to light only after their visitations were over. The printers in Charles Street, Chertsey, had a paranormal visitor who seems to have enjoyed fiddling with the controls on the printing machines, which led to a fair degree of mess, inconvenience and loss to the owners. The thing in the cellars of the Wheatsheaf pub in Croydon apparently liked to move bottles and boxes about, much to the annoyance of the landlady, but did no real damage. The Greyhound Inn at Lingfield had a

The poltergeist that plagued the Queens Head pub in Weybridge seems to have been a fairly typical example. It moved objects about and played a variety of practical tricks on the landlord for a period of some months, then faded away and has not been heard of since. The pub is now part of a chain of French restaurants.

poltergeist in the 1980s that moved small objects about, and one witness claimed to have seen the ghost of a young boy in Victorian clothes in the bar.

One of the best-documented poltergeists in all England visited a house in Stockwell in 1772. At the time, Stockwell was a Surrey village well outside London, though it has since been swallowed up by the urban sprawl. The visitation caused a sensation at the time and was investigated by several local gentlemen. The principal witnesses were Mary Golding, John Pain, Mary Pain, Richard Fowler and Sarah Fowler, who were persuaded to write down their accounts, which were then published as a pamphlet and sold well.

Mrs Golding was an elderly lady of independent means and it was in her house that the disturbances took place. With her lived her niece, Mary Pain, and her husband, John, who farmed nearby land before sending his produce to sale in London. The Pains had several children. Richard and Sarah Fowler lived in the next door house. The house on the other side was inhabited by the Greasham family. Mrs Golding had a live-in maid named Ann Robinson, who was about twenty years old. Neither the Greashams nor Robinson gave their accounts, which is a shame.

The poltergeist may have been performing smaller or less dramatic stunts for some time before it announced itself in dramatic fashion on 6 January 1772. Certainly Ann Robinson seems to have been convinced that the 'spirit' had been around for some time. Maybe she had experienced paranormal events that she had not reported to her employer. Be that as it may, at 10 a.m. that Monday morning a terrific crash came from the kitchen. Mrs Golding hurried in to see what had caused the noise. She found Robinson sat at the table peeling vegetables, while several plates from the sideboard lay smashed on the stone floor. Robinson said that the plates had jumped off the shelf by themselves. Mrs Golding told her not to be so ridiculous, at which point four more plates leapt from the shelf, hovered momentarily in the air and then fell to the floor and smashed. They were followed by a clock, a lantern and a dish on which sat a joint of beef. Mrs Golding ran next door to the Greasham house, where she fainted. Robinson followed, and told the Greashams what had happened.

Mr Greasham was out, so Mrs Greasham sent a child to run and fetch Mr and Mrs Pain from their work in nearby fields. She also sent for Dr Gardner. When he arrived, Dr Gardner decided to bleed Mrs Golding, who had by this time come round and was lying down in her bedroom. No sooner had he bled Mrs Golding, than the doctor leapt up in alarm. The blood was swirling around in its china bowl in a most unnatural way. Then the blood reared up in a solid column before leaping out of the bowl on to the floor. At this point, the bowl shattered into a hundred pieces. Dr Gardner fled the house.

Meanwhile, Mr and Mrs Pain were in the kitchen discussing what they should do. Just before they saw Dr Gardner leave in a hurry, they heard a strange scratching noise, as if invisible rats were about. Then mayhem broke out. Pots, pans and plates were thrown around the kitchen by unseen hands. Some smashed, others came to rest gently. With some courage, the Pains raced upstairs and grabbed Mrs Golding, dragging her out of the house and back to the Greashams.

They stayed there until 2 p.m., when Mr Greasham came home. He refused to believe the stories he was told and boldly went to the apparently haunted house. He found a scene of destruction. Not only were plates broken in the kitchen, but much of the furniture in the parlour had been smashed to matchwood. As he walked back into the kitchen, Mr Greasham saw a pewter jug rise from the sideboard and float gently down on to the floor. A second later the jug flipped upside down. Then an egg floated out of the pantry and was flung by invisible hands across the room. Mr Greasham left at this point to return home.

Robinson, the maid, volunteered to go back to the house to gather up some of Mrs Golding's personal possessions. She made her way through the destruction downstairs and went upstairs. She returned saying that nothing untoward had happened while she was in the house.

Word of the strange events had, however, got out. A small crowd gathered outside the house. They were soon rewarded by the sounds of smashing crockery and furniture coming from the house. There was also a series of thumping bangs so loud that some thought the house was about to collapse. A carpenter who was present said that the work he had seen done a few weeks earlier in the attic was substandard and that the house was sure to be rubble within minutes. That ensured that nobody was willing to enter the house, though the strange noises continued. Now and then people saw furniture floating past the windows as if being carried about the house by an invisible intruder.

Later that day the Fowlers arrived and together with the Pains and Greashams discussed what should be done. They decided to leave things until the next day and then send for the vicar. It was not to be. At five o'clock the next morning, the Greasham household, with Mrs Golding, the Pains and Robinson, were woken up by a series of terrific bangs, thumps and crashes coming from the empty house. The noise continued until dawn, when silence fell. The Pains and Robinson ventured back to find even more furniture smashed, hangings torn down and everything in a total mess. There then came a crash from the cellar. Mr Pain went down to find a nine-gallon cask of beer had just been upended, the bung removed and the beer flowing out. A pail of water that stood on the kitchen floor then began to boil and a box of candles fell from a shelf.

At this point, Robinson said that she was quitting her job to go home to her family. She ran up to her room, grabbed her belongings and marched off. By lunchtime nothing untoward seemed to have happened anew and Mrs Golding said that she was going home. The Fowlers went with her. Nothing happened as they entered the house, so they began the process of clearing up. That was the end of the affair and nothing else paranormal took place.

The Surrey poltergeist cases are typical in many ways. Recent studies have shown that a poltergeist visitation will often follow a set pattern. Events start in a low key with odd noises that are often reported as faults in the plumbing system, or as mice or birds in the attic or behind walls. These noises will get louder, progressing on to thumps and knocking noises. Physical manifestations then set in, with objects being moved about or going missing. Sometimes small objects will appear from nowhere. At first the objects are moved when nobody is present, but later the objects will be seen to float about. Often no damage is done to the objects, but in rare cases they are smashed or broken. In a very few cases, the thrown objects may hit a person, but they usually do no harm. Only rarely does a poltergeist hurt anyone. In rare and exceptional cases, the poltergeist starts to communicate. It may knock answers to questions – one knock for yes, two for no – or write messages. Some even develop voices that come from thin air. The activity usually lasts a few weeks, or months at most, before it begins to fade away. Manifestations take place less often or less violently. Finally, a few months after the poltergeist arrives, it leaves.

Investigators have noticed some interesting things about poltergeists. They almost invariably occur in a house or workplace where a person is under stress or is unhappy. That person is almost always aged between eleven and twenty-one and is more often a girl than a boy. It is very often the case that the poltergeist manifestations occur when that person is present in the room, and only rarely if they are away from the building. Investigators term such a person the 'focus'.

Opinion among researchers is divided as to what causes a poltergeist visitation. Some think that the focus person is inadvertently causing the manifestations. They postulate that the stress and emotional turmoil that they are under causes a telekinetic reaction that externalises the inner conflicts as random acts of mischief. Others believe that it is the emotional strains of the others in the house that collectively prompt telekinetic acts to centre on the focus person. Some researchers still subscribe to the theory that a poltergeist is a separate entity who is attracted by the focus person, perhaps finding in them a way to break through into the human world. These days nobody really takes the ideas of witchcraft, boggarts or ghosts seriously when it comes to poltergeists.

More rational scientists, however, point out that nobody has been able to demonstrate telekinetic ability convincingly, nor are disembodied entities known to exist. They prefer to dismiss poltergeists as nonsense. They claim that the youngsters who are the focus are mischievously faking the whole business, or that the adult witnesses have made things up. Those who have been on the receiving end of a poltergeist visitation, however, are only too convinced that the phenomenon is very real indeed. Paranormal and unable to be explained, perhaps, but nonetheless real for that.

NINE

CRISIS APPARITIONS

There is a whole class of paranormal events that is very often confused with ghosts and conventional hauntings, but which is generally reckoned by researchers to be something very different. These crisis apparitions may be characterised as ghosts that appear only once, though other investigators prefer to view them in terms of ESP (extrasensory perception) or clairvoyance. Surrey is a county that seems to have been particularly rich in such paranormal events.

In March 1920, the police in London received a call from a man named Gordon Tombe who said that he had reason to believe that his son had been killed in suspicious circumstances. Superintendent Carlin was sent to interview Tombe and came back with both a bizarre story of the paranormal and the basis for a complex fraud investigation.

Tombe told Carlin that his son, George Eric Tombe, had been missing for six weeks. The young man had been looking for a career after leaving the Army at the end of the First World War. After what proved to be a couple of false starts, he had decided to earn a living as a horse breeder. Young Tombe knew a fair amount about horses and was a gifted amateur jockey, but did not know much about the business side of such an enterprise. He therefore teamed up with a business partner named Ernest Dyer. Tombe would run the horse side of things and deal with clients, while Dyer handled the money and financial side. Tombe senior had not been happy with this proposal; he had apparently taken something of a dislike to Dyer. Father and son had an argument over the proposed business and their relationship had become rather strained, though they stayed in touch.

The two young men had raised the money to start their venture and had bought Welcomes Farm, Kenley. The farm has long since vanished under twentieth-century housing estates, but it stood on Hayes Lane, near what is now Fairways. Then the farm was fairly isolated, but surrounded by large areas of open downland that provided top-quality grazing for horses. Around £5,000 – then a substantial sum of money – was put into the business. At first, all seemed to be going well; young Tombe had little difficulty finding clients and had a good eye for horses, while Dyer seemed to be making a good job of the finances.

Then, while Tombe was in northern England on business, the farm was badly damaged by fire. Around £4,000 worth of damage was done, and Dyer then confessed that in order to save money he had skimped on fire insurance. Only half the loss would be made good, Dyer said. The two men moved into rented lodgings near the devastated farm while they tried to work out a plan to salvage their business. That was when Tombes had accidentally discovered that the fire insurance on the farm was actually for the sum of £12,000. He suspected Dyer of trying to pocket the difference and confronted him. Dyer had come up with some glib excuse, and Tombe had chosen to accept it – at least for as long as it took to get the money and arrange for the partnership to be ended. Tombe had visited his parents at this point to update them on the affair.

That had been the last time that Tombe's parents had seen him. A few weeks later they received a letter from him saying that the insurance company was withholding some of the payment while they investigated what they thought might have been arson. After that they had heard nothing. Tombe senior had written to the lodgings, only to be told by the owner that the two young men had moved out a few weeks earlier. Tombe went to Kenley to look for himself. He found the farm overgrown and abandoned, while the lodgings owner could tell him nothing except that the men had left without having given a forwarding address.

Carlin agreed that it all sounded rather suspicious, but could not see why Tombe and his wife believed their son was dead. He may have been more implicated in the arson and fraud than he had told them and decided to go into hiding. That was when Tombe told Carlin that his wife had had a vision in which she saw their son lying dead in a small, confined, dark place. The young man's head had been smashed in and was covered in blood, while his eyes were open. She got the impression that he was in an underground room or opening. Mrs Tombe was emphatic about what she had seen. It had not been a dream, it had been far to vivid for that. And she had somehow got from the vision the very firm impression that her son was dead.

Carlin left thinking that the woman was imagining things due to worry about her son, but convinced that there was a very real fraud to be investigated. He went to work, contacting the insurance company and inspecting the financial books of Welcomes Farm. Not only was the evidence for arson clear, but so was the fact that Dyer had been creaming off thousands of pounds of profits from the business and converting it into cash – all of which was missing. He issued a note to police all over Britain giving a description of Dyer and Tombe saying that they were wanted for fraud.

Three months later Carlin took a call from police in Scarborough. They had been alerted by a hotel to a young man passing dud cheques in the name of Eric Tombe. When they had gone to arrest the man, he had pulled out a gun and opened fire. As the police closed in, the man had shot himself and died some time later, having refused to answer any questions. The dead man matched Dyer's description, but there was no sign of Tombe. Having backtracked Dyer from Scarborough back to Kenley, Carlin realised that at no point had Tombe been with Dyer nor had he turned up anywhere else.

Carlin now decided to carry out a more rigorous search of the abandoned farm than he had done at first. A specialist search team was brought in and after a couple of days they found an old, covered-over well shaft. Lying at the foot of the well were the mouldering remains of young George Eric Tombe. His head had been smashed in exactly as his mother had described from her vision.

The Tombe case created a sensation at the time, as much for the mother's vision as for the gory details of the murder and fatal shootout in Scarborough. Other examples of apparitions being seen at the time of a person's death are less dramatic, but just as paranormal.

In 1932, the Reverend Mr Marshall of St Paul's Church, Woking, was taken ill. He was moved to hospital and a temporary replacement brought in to take up his ecclesiastical duties. A couple of days later a parishioner was in the church when she saw Marshall standing beside

In 1932 an apparition of the vicar of Woking's St Paul's Church was seen in the chancel at almost the exact moment that the man was dying in hospital.

the altar rail. She thought that he must have recovered rather quicker than expected and was back in the parish, but since he appeared to be deep in thought she did not bother him. It was not until a couple of days later that she heard that Marshall had died, and that he had breathed his last at about the time that she had seen him in the church.

A rather similar case occurred in Esher in the summer of 1812. The novelist Anna Maria Porter, whose novel *The Hungarian Brothers* had been published in 1807 to critical acclaim and high sales, was sitting reading in the parlour of her home at 85 High Street. The door to the room had then opened and a man who she knew well, but whose identity she chose to keep secret, walked in. He looked upset and distracted as he walked across the room, sat down in a chair, then leapt up again and stalked out. Porter called her maid to ask how the man had been able to get into the house without being properly announced, but the maid said that nobody had entered the house and that the door was locked.

Wondering if she had been dreaming, Porter summoned a boy and sent him running to the friend's house about a mile away to see if he had come to pay a visit and, if he had, why he had not stopped to talk. The boy came back some forty minutes later with the news that the man in question had suffered a sudden seizure and fallen down dead barely an hour earlier, which would have been about the time Porter had seen him in her house.

Rather more gruesome was the vision seen by a man in Guildford Prison in 1670. Space in the prison was obviously fairly limited as the man, imprisoned for robbery, was sharing a cell with a pair of newcomers who were awaiting trial. At about 1 a.m. the robber was startled awake by something, and confronted with a hideous apparition. Standing in the cell was an elderly man dressed in a dark coat and breeches. His throat had been slashed deeply, and a second wound in his chest was oozing blood. The man was bending over the two newcomers. He seemed to realise that the robber was awake, and turned to face him with a face of great melancholy. Then he vanished abruptly.

The shocked robber waited until dawn then hammered on the door of the cell and demanded to be moved to a different room. When asked why, he explained what had happened the night before. The gaoler took the robber to see the governor, who alone of those in Guildford knew that the two men who had been sharing the cell with the robber were in transit to stand trial for the murder of a man named Bower, who had been killed by two knife wounds that exactly matched those described by the robber.

There then followed a bizarre series of discussions between Mr Justice Reading, the judge taking the case, and the lawyers for prosecution and defence as to whether the robber's vision could be presented as evidence in court. In the end, Reading ruled that it was hearsay evidence and so was not admissible, neatly sidestepping the issue of whether a ghost could give evidence. The two men were found guilty of the murder on other evidence and hanged. Presumably the apparition of the unfortunate Mr Bower was content.

A rather more modern case comes from December 2002. Several motorists on the A3 at Burpham saw a car go out of control and veer off the road into a dense patch of roadside bushes. They pulled up and called police on their mobile phones. When the police arrived there was no sign at all of a crash, nor of any disturbance to the bushes. But the witnesses were insistent about what they had seen.

The A3 at Burpham was the site of a well-attested apparition in 2002 that was seen by at least half a dozen people, but has never been explained.

The police decided to investigate and pushed their way into the thicket. They were surprised to find a crashed car, but it had become overgrown by weeds and had quite obviously been there for some months, not half an hour or so as the witnesses were insisting. Sitting at the wheel of the car was a skeleton. The gruesome find sparked an investigation. Fortunately, the number plate of the car was quickly traced. It belonged to a man who had been reported missing by his family six months earlier.

It was presumed that the man had been killed on the day he went missing, but that nobody had seen the car crash. The vehicle and its gruesome driver had then sat hidden in the thicket until discovered. What nobody could explain was what the motorists had seen that convinced them a car had crashed when, in fact, no such accident had taken place that day at all.

The most famous Surrey case of an apparition being seen on the point of death occurred in Epsom in November 1779. The main character in the drama was Lord Thomas Lyttleton, a notoriously debauched young man of enormous wealth and depraved habits. In the autumn of 1778, Lyttleton was visiting friends in Worcestershire when he chanced upon a widow by the name of Mrs Amphlett. This Mrs Amphlett had been left with three young daughters by her husband; Elizabeth, aged fifteen, Christianna, aged seventeen, and Margaret, aged nineteen. All three girls were considered to be most pretty and since Mrs Amphlett had been left a fair-sized fortune, it was assumed by all in Worcestershire that the girls would soon make good marriages.

Mrs Amphlett was understandably upset and concerned when Lord Lyttleton began to pay attention to the girls. His behaviour was notorious and she was determined to protect her daughters. Lyttleton, however, behaved impeccably throughout his time in Worcestershire. He visited the Amphletts, but only when the mother was present, attended church and lived as soberly and free of gambling as anyone could expect.

However, things were not as they seemed. When Lord Lyttleton left for London in the spring, all three of the girls went with him – without telling their mother where they were going. The gossip in London was that Lyttleton had seduced all three, while the more lewd tales were of four-in-a-bed romps. The scandal was immense, and the news broke the health of poor Mrs Amphlett.

On 25 November, Lord Lyttleton was hosting a house party at his London residence in Berkeley Square. At the party were the three Misses Amphlett, Lord Fortescue, Lady Flood and Captain Wolseley. That morning, Lyttleton was late down to breakfast. When he did appear he was pale and ill at ease. During the night he had awoken with a start to see a white bird flying around his room. As he watched in horrified fascination, the bird had landed and grown to assume the shape of a middle-aged woman in a pale night gown.

'You must prepare to leave this world,' said the woman, 'and join me in the next'.

'Not soon,' stammered Lyttleton.

'Yes,' came the chilling reply. 'In three days.' Then the woman had faded from sight.

Lyttleton's friends tried to make light of the event, saying it was just a bad dream. Lyttleton, however, remained morose and depressed. It had been no dream, he insisted, it had been a vision unlike anything he had ever experienced before. To try to cheer him up one of the girls suggested that they should go to Lyttleton's house, Pitt Place, in Epsom. The house stood on Burgh Heath Road that led from the town centre up to the downs where horse races were, and still are, run. It is commemorated today in the name of the residential road, Pitt Road.

One of the most famous of all apparitions linked to a sudden death centred around Pitt Place in Epsom, home of the dissolute Lord Lyttleton. The grand house was demolished in the twentieth century and replaced with a number of smaller houses, as shown here.

Once in Epsom, Lyttleton seemed to cheer up. The three young women certainly did all they could to raise his spirits, as the valet was to make clear in his account of what happened next. On the third day after his vision, Lyttleton was out and about in Epsom, cheerfully telling his horse racing cronies that he would 'bilk' the phantom messenger – gambler's slang for having cheated on a bet. Just to make sure, he dropped in on his doctor. The doctor was unable to find anything wrong with him, but prescribed a general tonic of rhubarb and mint with instructions that it was to be diluted with water. Lyttleton spent that evening at Pitt Place alone with the Amphlett girls.

The valet was summoned to Lyttleton's room at around 10 p.m. – after the girls had left – to prepare his lordship for bed. Lyttleton ordered breakfast to be served at 8 a.m., then picked up the tonic. He asked the valet to fetch him a spoon to stir the syrup into a glass of water. The valet walked down to the kitchen to get a spoon and, on his return, found Lyttleton writhing on the bedroom floor choking and coughing. The valet shouted loud, rousing the girls from their adjacent room and sent them to get a footman to run for the doctor. The valet lifted Lyttleton and struck him on the back, thinking that he might be choking on a piece of food. The efforts had no noticeable effect. A few moments later, Lyttleton went rigid, shook spasmodically and died.

At that moment, a friend of Lyttleton's named Miles Andrews was himself preparing for bed having returned from an evening out. He happened to glance toward his open bedroom door and saw Lyttleton wandering past clad in nightshirt and nightcap. Thinking that his old friend had recovered from his melancholy and was back in London, he went outside to talk to him. Lyttleton was nowhere in sight, so Andrews summoned a servant to ask which room Lyttleton had been given and why he had not been told that his friend was staying. The servant denied that Lyttleton or anyone else unexpected was in the house. Puzzled, Andrews went to bed to sleep off his evening's meal. The next day he woke up to a hangover and a message announcing the death of his friend.

What was already a fairly bizarre tale of the paranormal took a fresh turn for the even more dramatic two days later. A messenger came riding up to Pitt Place on a tired horse asking for the Amphlett ladies. He brought with him a letter from their uncle giving them the sad news that their mother had passed away at 3 a.m. five days earlier – at almost the exact time that Lyttleton had had his vision of a woman in a night dress summoning him to his death.

TEN

UFOs

People have been reporting odd things in the skies for centuries. The detail and reliability of these reports vary a great deal, but together they give the impression that someone or something was flying through the air long before humans worked out how to do it. These sorts of reports have been found in chronicles, manuscripts and histories across Europe and Asia – almost anywhere that people were able to write down accounts of unusual sights.

It was, however, only after humans had learnt how to fly that the reports began to be taken seriously. Instead of assuming the objects were dragons, fairies or gods, witnesses began to worry that they might be foreign war machines and so took rather more notice of them. In 1897, for instance, sightings of what were thought to be airships were made over North America. The 'airships' flew faster and higher than any known airship made by humans.

By 1912 the people of Surrey had very real reason to worry about what was flying over their heads. Tensions with Germany were rising and would lead to the outbreak of the First World War only two years later. Everyone knew that the Germans had a fleet of military airships, termed Zeppelins after their inventor, equipped to fly long distances either to drop bombs or scout out enemy military positions. It was with some alarm, therefore, that British civilians learned that 'airships' had been sighted coming in from over the sea to fly over ports such as Liverpool, Dover and Harwich. Then the 'airships' began to be seen inland, including over Surrey.

At the time, it was assumed that these were craft belonging to a foreign military force – the German Navy was the favourite suspect – but the descriptions given of the 'airships' made it clear that they were not much like contemporary flying machines. They were of an elongated oval shape and, when seen in daylight, had a smooth surface much like Zeppelins. There were, however, no visible engines, nor a cabin or gondola as might be expected. More bizarrely, the craft glowed at night as if illuminated from within by a bright, throbbing electric light. Moreover, they sometimes left behind a trail of grey or brown smoke. At least one was accompanied by smaller, brightly illuminated round objects that seemed to swirl and swoop around it. Questions were raised in the House of Commons and Winston Churchill, then First Lord of the Admiralty, assured MPs that there was no evidence that the strange flying objects were hostile German war machines, though that did leave open the question of what they in fact were.

Winston Churchill, shown here in RAF uniform during the Second World War, was forced to answer questions about a series of UFO sightings in the House of Commons.

The next few decades were quiet over Surrey, though strange flying objects were reported elsewhere. It was in 1947 that the real interest in these mysterious objects took off. On 24 June, American businessman Kenneth Arnold was flying home from a meeting in his private aircraft when he spotted some strange objects flying over the Mount Rainier area of Washington State in the USA. The nine objects flew at an astonishing speed, which, as an experienced pilot, Arnold knew to be quite impossible for contemporary aircraft. He watched them, fearing that they might be top secret Soviet intruders. He noticed that they moved with a strange, undulating motion that he later likened to that followed by a saucer skipping over water. The term 'flying saucer' was born.

The report dominated headlines across the USA, then the world and led to a rash of reports from people who had seen similar 'flying saucers'. In Britain, attention focussed on the Wiltshire town of Warminster, where sightings of flying saucers seemed to be particularly numerous. Gradually, the focus shifted as reports began to come in from other counties, including Surrey. As the years passed it began to become clear that the term 'flying saucer' did not do justice to the range of shapes and sizes of the mysterious flying objects. The term 'Unidentified Flying Object', or UFO, began to be used instead. There were also an increasing number of sightings of what seemed to be occupants emerging from UFOs. These beings were generally humanoid in that they had two legs, two arms and one head, but they tended to be fairly small, typically around 3 or 4ft tall. They were generally shy of humans, preferring to land and emerge in remote rural areas or in the early hours of the morning when people were unlikely to be about. The beings would usually flee if humans turned up, though sometimes they used what seemed to be weapons able to stun a person. Just occasionally, a person was apparently abducted by them to be subjected to weird and often painful experiments.

Such disturbing encounters have, thankfully, not been reported in Surrey. But one other aspect of the UFO phenomenon has been that of 'flaps'. A UFO flap occurs when a large number of UFO sightings are made within a relatively short space of time and from a restricted geographical area. Why these flaps occur is a mystery, and the solution has much to do with what the UFOs themselves might be.

With hindsight, the Surrey flap of 2007-08 probably got underway on the Easter weekend of 2007. At 9.30 p.m., a large object was seen over the Hogs Back, west of Guildford. The object seemed to be rather insubstantial, almost as if it were composed of shifting, glowing gas instead of being a solid, flying mechanical craft. The object gave off an intensely bright orange light for some minutes before fading from view.

A few weeks later (the precise date was not recorded as the witness did not come forward until some months later), another UFO was spotted over Worplesdon. This object was rather more conventional, being disc-shaped and silvery-grey in colour. It flew silently over the Jolly Farmer pub.

In June, a round, red object was sighted flying over Addiscombe. The witness saw it for only a few seconds and was unable to give a clear description of the craft.

On 5 August a UFO was spotted flying over Croydon in the early afternoon. A young couple were in Shirley Road when they saw a round, white object heading north. They at first took it for a helicopter, until they realised that it was moving in complete silence. Looking more closely, they saw that it was a smooth, oval shape with no obvious wings, rotors or other protuberances. They estimated that the object was rather larger than a van and that it was moving quite fast in a straight line.

The next sighting came on 15 September at Wonersh. It was 10.30 p.m. when a group of eight UFOs came into sight. They were arranged in pairs, with a single light at front and rear. The lights were steady, not flashing like those of aircraft, and far too bright to be stars. They were heading toward the north-west in complete silence. They flew on without changing direction until they were out of sight.

On Christmas Day 2007 another sighting took place, this time at Effingham. It was about 7 p.m. when three spherical objects were seen coming from the north. The witness called his family out into the garden to watch, so that in all five people saw the lights. The lights were much brighter than those of the aircraft often seen overhead in the area. The three glowing balls of light were heading south-west. They remained visible for almost three minutes before vanishing from sight.

The very next day, another sighting was made north of Guildford. The weather was dull and a thick blanket of cloud blocked out the stars and high-flying aircraft. At 9 p.m. a man slipped out of his house to smoke a cigarette in the garden. He then saw a flame-coloured round light approaching from the south. The man watched the object fly silently through the sky, puzzled by what it could be. Just as he was finishing his cigarette he saw a second, identical object in the southern sky. He called a friend out to watch and together they saw this new intruder repeat the flight path of the first. Both objects were flying underneath the clouds, and so could not have been stars or other natural objects. The witness recalled that there was a very gentle breeze at the time and that the objects were going in the same direction, but much faster.

Unusual in that it happened in bright daylight in the middle of the afternoon was the sighting of 15 May from Malden. A young woman was in her garden when her partner pointed out to her a bright orange object high up in the sky. The craft seemed to be perfectly spherical and to be flying toward the south. As the pair watched the object, it picked up speed and zoomed off out of sight.

A mass sighting took place on 31 May 2008 at Normandy, when no fewer than twenty objects were seen by two witnesses in clear conditions. It was late evening when one of the witnesses left her house to drive to Guildford to collect a friend from the railway station. She glanced up and saw a number of spherical orange lights strung out in a line across the sky.

They were moving slowly forward, with the leading objects fading from view as they reached a particular spot in the sky. Another person also saw the objects, and when the two witnesses compared notes later, they found that their descriptions tallied exactly.

As the summer of 2008 passed by, the number of sightings picked up – perhaps because more people were outside in the warmer weather. The sighting of 16 July from Thames Ditton was typical of several made around this time. It was about 9 p.m. on an overcast day with high and broken clouds. The witness reported that the object was perfectly round with a shiny red surface. It was quite low when first seen, perhaps only three times as high as the top of the house. The witness pointed the object out to her husband and together they watched it change direction so that it was climbing almost straight up to disappear into the clouds. About an hour later a second object appeared; this time it was of a silver colour and was gliding silently in a horizontal direction. The object was in sight for only a few seconds before it vanished behind some trees. 'It did not look like anything I had ever seen before and cannot explain what it was,' concluded the witness

On 4 January 2009 the flap was drawing to a close, but that did not stop a series of UFOs being sighted over Guildford. The sighting took place just past midnight as the witness drove along Cabell Road. Two orange lights appeared in the sky, causing the witness to stop his car and peer out. Two more lights joined the first two as they approached silently. Three of the lights formed a triangular formation, while the fourth was off to one side. As the lights got closer they seemed to be round balls of fire. They passed by without making any sound and vanished into the distance.

There was a brief final flurry of activity before the Surrey flap ended completely. Godstone was the scene for a sighting on the evening of 28 February. The witness spotted six orange balls of light hovering overhead. He went to get a friend to show them to him, but in the few moments that he was not watching them, the UFOs vanished from sight. When the sighting was made public, a second witness came forward to confirm that he too had seen the glowing balls of light that evening. This new witness had seen the lights in Oxted, and reported that they were flying fairly fast overhead.

On 25 May, a large spherical object emitting an orange light was seen over Caterham. The couple who reported the object were first alerted by the odd behaviour of their German Shepherd dog, which seemed to be suddenly unsettled and kept peering upward at the sky. Looking up, they saw what appeared to be an orange globe pulsating with light. The object flew across the sky to disappear into the gathering gloom of evening.

What all these sightings have in common is that they are frustratingly short on detail, as is the case with most UFO sightings. The witnesses are adamant that they have seen something highly unusual and quite unlike anything that they have ever seen before. Exactly what that something is remains unclear as the object was seen at some distance or for only a few seconds. Very different was the sighting made by Alfred Burtoo on the banks of the Basingstoke Canal, just west of Ash Wharf, in August 1983.

Mr Burtoo lived in the North Town area of Aldershot, just over the border in Hampshire, and was a keen angler. He particularly liked to fish the waters of the canal at night when few other people were about and the area was quiet and still. He usually took his dog, Tiny, along for company and set up camp on the towpath around midnight to stay until dawn, or until he had had enough.

Above left: Effingham was the scene of a sighting of multiple UFOs on Christmas Day 2007.

Above right: A resident of Cabell Road in Guildford reported seeing a UFO in January 2009.

This particular night began like any other that Burtoo had spent on the canalside. He heard the clock strike 1 a.m. and some minutes later he poured a hot cup of tea out of his Thermos flask. That was when he sighted an odd light in the sky. The bright illumination seemed to be coming from a round or oval object rather larger than an aircraft. The object came towards him, emitting a high-pitched whine. It came to a halt when about 300yds away, then began to descend with a rocking motion. It disappeared out of sight behind some trees to the west in the direction of the railway line. The illumination then went out. Puzzled, but not unduly worried, Burtoo took a sip of tea.

That was when Tiny began to growl. Looking back to the west, Burtoo could see two human-like figures coming toward him along the towpath. Burtoo ordered his dog to be silent, whereupon it slunk down, keeping its master between itself and the approaching figures. Burtoo stood up to greet the newcomers and as they got closer realised that they were both much shorter than him; he later estimated them to have been around 4ft tall.

The two figures appeared to be almost identical. They were fairly slender, but not abnormally so. Both were wearing tight green overalls that covered them from neck to foot. Burtoo did not recall what sort of footwear they had on, but thought that their hands were bare. The overalls were of a smooth fabric that had a sheen to it, which Burtoo thought was perhaps some form of plastic. The heads of both humanoids were covered in near-spherical helmets which featured a black visor covering the eye area. Nothing could be seen of their heads or faces.

The two beings came to within a few feet of Burtoo, who stood up to face them. The humanoids then stood facing Burtoo as if studying him closely. Then one of them beckoned Burtoo to follow and turned around to start walking back along the towpath. Feeling neither fear nor anxiety, Burtoo followed. The second being fell in behind him so that the three of them were walking in single file, west toward the railway line.

The canalside towpath near Ash Wharf, where Surrey's most spectacular UFO sighting took place in 1983.

When they reached Government Road bridge, the path went through a gate, over the road, through a second gate and then back to the canal side. Burtoo remembered that the first being went through the gates, apparently without opening them. He recalled he had to open the gates to pass through himself and that the leading humanoid was already on the other side as he did so.

Back on the towpath, Burtoo could now see the object that he had earlier glimpsed coming in to land. He estimated it to be around 45ft across and to be perfectly smooth and oval in shape. There were what looked like round windows around the rim of the object, and it rested on two legs. It was resting on the towpath, with part of it projecting out over the canal waters. A hatch or door opened and steps emerged as the little procession approached.

Burtoo followed the lead creature up the steps into the craft. Inside, the walls were completely smooth, merging into the floor and ceiling with smooth curves so that there were no corners anywhere. He was then led through a doorway into another room. The second humanoid stopped in the doorway, blocking Burtoo's route out of the craft should he choose to try to leave.

For about ten minutes the first being busied itself with what appeared to be controls of some kind. Two other humanoids entered the room to join the first in operating the controls. There was a shaft from floor to ceiling of the chamber; one of the beings stood close to a handle or control on this shaft at all times, as if to stop Burtoo from touching it.

Finally, the beings seemed to finish whatever they were doing. A voice boomed out from somewhere telling Burtoo to stand under the amber light. Burtoo could not see any such light at first, but then saw it high up on a wall, close to the ceiling. He did as asked, and was quickly bathed in a soft orange light. After about five minutes the light switched itself off and the voice returned.

'What is your age?' it asked.

'I'm seventy-eight,' responded Burtoo.

There was a pause, then the voice said, 'You can go. You are too old for our purposes.'

One of the humanoids waved Burtoo toward the door out of the chamber, led him across the outer room and pointed down the steps. Burtoo walked down the steps and retreated several yards along the towpath before turning to look back at the object. The steps were gone, the door closed and the dome on top of the craft appeared to be turning slowly. Burtoo then returned to his fishing spot. Spotting his cup of tea, now cold, Burtoo decided to finish it while he thought about what had just happened to him.

As he pondered in the darkness, Burtoo heard the same whine that had accompanied the arrival of the object. Looking to the west, Burtoo saw the object rising back into the air. It hovered briefly, then accelerated rapidly away toward the west until it was out of sight. Burtoo looked at his watch. It was now 2 a.m., about forty minutes or so after he had first seen the craft approaching. Unsure what to do, Burtoo sat down to carry on fishing while he thought about his experience and what he should do.

The eyewitness to the sighting in 1983 reported that the two figures that emerged from the UFO walked up this path, bearing right beside the bridge to cross the road.

A couple of hours later, two policemen from the nearby military camp came along to check up on who the figure hunched by the canal was. Burtoo told them about what had happened. One of the policemen grinned. 'I expect they were checking on our military installations,' he said. Burtoo could not tell if he was joking or being serious. Either way, the policemen moved off.

Burtoo packed up and went home. He told his wife about his experience, but at first nobody else. Then he fell ill with nausea, diarrhoea and prolonged lethargy. It was this that caused him to report the encounter and seek medical aid. The symptoms cleared up after a couple of weeks, but nobody was ever able to give Alfred Burtoo a satisfactory explanation for what had happened to him.

The Burtoo encounter was one of the very few in which a witness has encountered the occupants of a UFO, and even entered the craft itself. Most UFO sightings are of objects in the sky, though sometimes seen at very close quarters and in considerable detail. The incident raises more questions than it settles. Taken at face value, it would indicate that UFOs are mechanical flying craft operated by diminutive humanoid creatures of intelligence. On the other hand, nothing reported by Mr Burtoo indicated where these beings had come from nor what sort of life form they were. Still less clear was why they landed on the towpath of Ash Wharf that particular night. All Mr Burtoo could gather was that he was too old for their purposes, whatever they were.

The ideas put forward to explain UFOs are many, and some are more sensible than others. The most widespread idea among scientists is that most sightings are, in fact, of perfectly normal objects but seen in unusual circumstances, so that they are not recognised for what they are. When an object is seen fleetingly and at a distance, this is a real possibility and there can be no doubt that a great many UFO reports can be explained in this way.

However, some sightings are at very close distances, or involved witnesses actually touching or entering the UFO itself. These cannot be dismissed as mistaken identity. Instead, scientists doubt whether the person is telling the truth, or allege that the supposed sighting is a hallucination or waking dream. Some aspects of the Burtoo sighting might support this case. Nobody saw the UFO or its occupants other than himself, and the way the first humanoid passed through the gate without opening it does sound rather like a dream. On the other hand, Mr Burtoo did suffer some very real sickness in the days that followed, as have others who have encountered a UFO at close quarters.

The explanation most favoured by those researching UFOs is that they are spacecraft bringing aliens to Earth. Opinions differ as to why the aliens are visiting our planet. Some think that they are basically friendly or, at worst, disinterested observers. Other researchers fear they are hostile and cite cases of people being abducted to support their case. It must be admitted that there is no real evidence that the UFOs are spacecraft, nor that their occupants are aliens. Most 'aliens' are no more informative than those met by Burtoo. There are a few instances of UFO occupants explaining to the human witness that they are aliens from another planet, but who is to say that the humanoids are telling the truth? Maybe the alien story is put about to hide the real truth – whatever that may be.

Finally, it must be said that the whole subject of UFOs and aliens is rife with hoaxes, trickery and practical jokes. On 31 March 1989 one such stunt caused widespread alarm in Surrey. The first sign of trouble came in the afternoon when police received a call from a woman living near South Godstone to say that a flying saucer was hovering over her house. The telephonist responded calmly, asking the woman for a description. The woman was clearly agitated, but was able to explain that the object was bigger than her house, was round with a dome on top and a row of windows around the rim. It was, she said, now moving very slowly north.

What the woman did not explain, because she was unaware of the fact, was that she was standing in the doorway of her house totally naked. She was so amazed by the object overhead that she had forgotten that she was getting changed to go out. Only when a neighbour shouted across to her did the woman realise her situation and dash back inside.

Next to call in was a motorist on the M25 near Limpsfield. He was using the emergency roadside telephone, which was usually reserved for breakdowns, to report a huge UFO overhead heading toward London. Then a second motorist called in, this time on a car phone, to report the same thing. Convinced that something odd was happening, the telephonist alerted a police car in the area and sent it to investigate.

The police car arrived to find several vehicles stationary on the hard shoulder of the M25 as the occupants stood about staring into the sky to the north. The police followed their stares and were amazed to see a large, disc-shaped object that looked exactly like the popular image of a flying saucer. It was silver, had portholes or windows around the outer edge and was topped by a dome, also bearing windows. The object was huge, estimated at around 90ft across, and was quite clearly descending to land.

The policemen sprang back into their car and raced off toward the landing site. They arrived to find that the 'UFO' was in fact a hot air balloon specially commissioned to look like a flying saucer by the billionaire businessman Richard Branson. The balloon was being test flown for an April Fool Day's stunt in London's Hyde Park the following day.

The billionaire businessman Richard Branson was inadvertently responsible for sparking off a UFO scare in Surrey in 1989 when a practical joke went wrong.

Other local titles published by The History Press

Paranormal West Yorkshire
ANDY OWENS

With famous cases such as the Cottingley Fairies – investigated, of course, by Sir Arthur Conan Doyle – now forgotten cases such as the Pontefract Poltergeist and eye-witness accounts of ghosts, black cats and UFOs, this richly illustrated collection covers a fascinating range of strange events from West Yorkshire's history. Including sources both ancient and modern and with never-before published investigations by the Haunted Yorkshire Psychical Research Group, this book will delight all lovers of the unexplained.

978 0 7524 4810 7

Paranormal Edinburgh
GORDON RUTTER

Edinburgh's history spans hundreds of years and with such a long, rich, gruesome and incredible past it is no surprise that Scotland's capital city boasts an array of paranormal activity. Both ancient and modern, Edinburgh is a city of contrasts. Beneath its cosmopolitan veneer lies an extensive world of paranormal activity. From tales of ancient and modern-day witches, to fairy portals and ghostly sightings in the Old Town, this incredible volume will invite the reader to view this historic city in a whole new light. Illustrated with fifty intriguing pictures, *Paranormal Edinburgh* will delight all those interested in the mysteries of the paranormal.

978 0 7524 4974 6

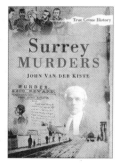

Surrey Murders
JOHN VAN DER KISTE

Surrey Murders is an examination of some of the county's most notorious and shocking cases. They include the 'Wigwam Girl', Joan Wolfe, who lived in a tent built by a Cree Indian Soldier before being brutally slaughtered; the infamous stabbing of Frederick Gold by 'the Serpent' Percy Lefroy Mapleton; the poisoning of the entire Beck family with a bottle of oatmeal stout laced with cyanide; and the sailor butchered at the Devil's Punch Bowl, later immortalised in Charles Dickens' *Nicholas Nickleby*. John Van der Kiste's carefully researched, well-illustrated and enthralling text will appeal to all those interested in the darker side of Surrey's history.

978 0 7509 5130 2

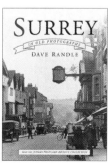

Surrey in Old Photographs
DAVE RANDLE

Judges Postcards have been celebrating the British landscape for over a hundred years. Their archive has now become a unique and priceless record of a century of change and this book draws on it to present a superb selection of images of Surrey's past. The sheer quality of Judges' photography combines with the author's informative and entertaining commentary to create an essential addition to the bookshelf, an ideal gift, and a surprisingly comprehensive introduction to the county.

978 0 7509 4161 7

Visit our website and discover thousands of other History Press books.

www.thehistorypress.co.uk